The Hockey Dynamic

Examining the Forces That Shaped the Modern Game

by Gavin Featherstone

REEDSWAIN PUBLISHING

88 Wells Road
Spring City, PA 19475
USA

**Library of Congress
Cataloging - in - Publication Data**

The Hockey Dynamic : Examining the Forces That Shaped the Modern Game
by Gavin Featherstone

ISBN-13: 9781591642381
Library of Congress Control Number: 2015934166
© 2015

Art Direction and Layout
Bryan R. Beaver

Photos:
Special Thanks to:
OBO (photos by Frank M.L. Uijlenbroek)
The Hockey Museum, Woking, England
The Australian Sports Commission
Ed Milner ; Private Collection

Reedswain Publishing
88 Wells Road
Spring City, PA 19475
www. reedswain.com
orders@reedswain.com

Contents

Foreword v

Preface vii

Part A - Asian Demise 1

Part B - The Old Boys Network 17

Part C - The AstroTurf Revolution 33

Part D - The Future is Video 49

Part E - Coaches Take the Lead 67

Part F - SuperClubs 83

Part G - Institutes and Academies 103

Part H - Logging, Foam and Moonboots 119

Part I - Play By the Rules 133

Part J - Hockey's Risk Takers 151

Part K - Hockey's New Shangri-La 173

Index 187

Bibliography 191

Dedicated to Charlie, Edie and the World's Hockey family.
- GAV

Foreword

I first met Gav at the England Schoolboys U18 trials in St Albans. He was selected as centre half and I was right half. Thus started a relationship that has lasted over 40 years. We played together again in England's U22 and England Seniors before Gav suffered from a severe knee injury that effectively ended his playing career.

Never one to let the grass grow under his feet, Gav moved into coaching and we next competed against each other at the Los Angeles Olympics in 1984 – Gav as Head coach of the USA Men's team and me as captain of GB Men's team. Gav's coaching career has spanned 4 continents and recently his work as Director of Hockey at Durham University has received much acclaim. Up in Durham he turned an average social University group into a highly organised professionally run performance unit. Many successes followed on the pitch.

Why oh why England and GB have not recruited his skills more remains a mystery. Maybe it is Gav's approach. He calls it as he sees it. This often does not go down well with the authorities but you always know where you stand with him and being a straight talking Yorkshireman I admire him for that. Maybe our leaders felt that they could not "control" him as he certainly has a bit of Brian Clough in his style.

But Gav has been able to give so much to fellow coaches. He has done many presentations for me to North and Commonwealth games coaches and his series of video training films were ground breaking and much sought after by coaches across the globe. He is an inspiring speaker with his thought provoking messages.

I hope that you enjoy reading this book. For sure you will read a no holds barred message from a guy who has been there and done that at all levels and areas within hockey.

Hockey is a better sport thanks to characters like Gavin and this book will give you an interesting perspective of the modern game and its development.

Enjoy the read

Norman Hughes
Former England and GB Captain
Olympic Bronze Medalist 1984
Current European Hockey Federation Education and Development Manager

Author's Preface

After celebrating 50 years since I first picked up a dirty old second hand Punjab Prince hockey stick off a classroom shelf in London, I decided to leave film as a means of communication and return to basics as we coaches would put it, and trace the incredible changes that have influenced the sport of hockey during that period.

"The Hockey Dynamic" is not about players, it is wholeheartedly about what lies behind the modern hockey player. Of all the world's team sports, hockey has made the most momentous changes over the last half century. I have tried to illustrate the most dynamic of these that have made it a faster, more skillful and more visual game fit for the twenty first century.

My father always warned me never to write or spout about areas of life that I have not directly experienced myself. Five decades in hockey have catapulted me from playing, to a host of other connected parts of the sport that were intrinsically linked to its progression. It has been a tremendous journey throughout all five continents.

Once investigations had started on the subject, I was soon to realise that it was to be a labour of love. Firstly, I had been directly caught up in many of the themes that had hit the game like a hurricane over these years. The eleven chapters correspond to a very solid, but dynamic team, and like any good hockey team, they interact and evolve to make a tremendous whole. Indeed it was straightforward to measure the subject areas where I had played a role, but it became a new ball game when I had to pursue the mass of processes, innovations and characters that had remained largely in the shadows of this half century.

Moreover, these challenges became all the more enjoyable as I was to venture across the hockey world, from Pittsburgh to Palmerston North, from Nairobi to Nashville, from Cape Town to Canberra and from Barcelona to Bloemendaal in search of the men and women that have moulded hockey into the entertaining modern game we all know today. Their stories, previously untold in detail, are central to the narrative as they fought for changes to expand and improve the game. What did the processes, innovations, risks and these personalities have in common --- They were all dynamic, Hockey Dynamic. After they had all cast their spell on one of the most established of Olympic sports, the game of hockey was never to be the same again as introduced in Chapter 1 of this book. It just got better and better !!

-Part A-

Asian Demise

"Auschlag, Hand Stop, Schlage!!" Michael Krause had completed the simple task of scoring the only goal in the Olympic final to give West Germany the gold in 1972. Even then, he did not realise he had delivered the passing shot to a forty-year dominance of Asian hockey.

This time in Munich, it was Pakistan's turn to be humbled, and they did not like it one bit. For hockey, there were incredible scenes at the medals ceremony where the FIH President Renee Frank was drenched with water thrown from the Pakistan bench along with players on the podium hurling their silver medals to the ground. The resultant FIH decision to ban the Asian giant from future competition for three years sent shock waves through the hockey world.

Without doubt, this defeat to a European upstart was truly the turning point in International hockey, which for India and Pakistan would herald a marked decline in not just their ability to win world tournaments, but also in the internal status of the sport to the subcontinent's masses.

To understand modern hockey, how important it is to be familiar with its history in the former British Raj, through the partition years to the enlargement of the sport to a world-wide game in the 1970s. The Pakistanis were well aware that in Munich they had opened the door for European success in the future. This very fact was reinforced the following year when Germany's tiny neighbour Holland won the World Cup in Amsterdam. The big question at this pivotal point in hockey history was whether it was a dynamic rise in European standards or, indeed, the demise of Asian hockey.

Since 1928 when the Netherlands had grasped the mantle to host Olympic hockey, India (note that this included modern Pakistan and Bangladesh and the British military based in the subcontinent) had won gold in six successive Olympiads with Pakistan triumphant in 1960, and again in Mexico in 1968. Throughout the pre-war years, Britain had co-opted the multitalented indigenous population of players into the Army and other vital services where players like Dhyan Chand, Rupe Singh and Shahahuddin would mix with the officer class of the Brits to effectively produce a modern equivalent of a professional squad. The progression towards a greater inclusion of native Indian players was very marked between the Olympic teams of 1928 and 1936. There was no political lobbying in those days, only pure ability triumphed as the British officer class dwindled in numbers at Hitler's Games in Berlin.

The Indian Army team would tour the country competing in internal tournaments, paralleled to the Gymkanas of Polo, across this vast country from the Punjab in the north to Madras and Calcutta in the south. The competitions would last for a week involving Banks, Railways, Civil Service, and later, the Airlines squads. Huge numbers of talented players would enroll in these government institutions as a means of creating a long term career as proficiency on the hockey, cricket or polo field often had resulted in promotion through the ranks to successful desk jobs on retirement.

Indeed, Dhyan Chand, the hockey wizard, to be compared to football's Pele, was very soon to be Major Chand. His exploits on the field were legendary. Between 1928 and 1948 as an attacking inside forward, he was a prolific provider and goal scorer all rolled into one.

Date	Olympic Venue	Gold Medalist
1928	Amsterdam	INDIA
1932	Los Angeles	INDIA
1936	Berlin	INDIA
(WWII)	--	--
1948	London	INDIA
1952	Helsinki	INDIA
1956	Melbourne	INDIA
1960	Rome	PAKISTAN
1964	Tokyo	INDIA
1968	Mexico City	PAKISTAN
1972	Munich	WEST GERMANY

Wherever Dhyan Chand played in India he was worshipped as a true champion of the sport and his legacy lasted well past retirement as he was the inspiration behind the continued success of the Asian teams in the later 50s and 60s decades. Throughout India in the major centres, you will come across several statues of the little wizard in public places. The author of these papers had recourse to his brilliance when listening in 1984 to an American survivor from the Los Angeles Games of 1932. Bill Boddington was a cult hero in United States field hockey folklore as he had dared to score against Major Chand's India. However, India had shaded the game by 24 goals to 1!! When asked about the dexterity and genius of India's playmaker, Bill just shook his head, smiled, opened his palms and said , "I've never seen anything like him since."

India's influence as the heartbeat of hockey spread rapidly through the British Empire. It was not just in the playing of the game, but India provided a central focus to early technology in the manufacture of hockey sticks and equipment to many team sports. Indigenous small scale industries were established, notably in the Punjab in cities like Jalandhar and Sialkot, where artisans carved the original shapes from ash trees which became hockey sticks and cricket bats for use all the world over.

This was highly significant, as inevitably, as the game progressed, technical improvements to the stick shape were to be revolutionised in these cottage industries. Even though the British Colonels and Majors preferred the long "English heads" which accentuated the hitting and stopping of the ball on the open side of the stick, the Asian players' quick hands and mobility of feet (note 'feet' as many of the Indian players played in bare feet!) necessitated a shorter stick head which could in turn develop the rapid fire reverse stick skills associated with Asian players.

These technological modifications would really kick in during these decades as British players rigidly stuck to their long extended heads. Wherever you played against an Indian on the field, he could simply change direction of the stick head at will, and bamboozle the colonial masters with quick hands, fakes, and stick deception. Here was born Britain's obsession with technical skills only belonging to the open side of the hockey stick. Even by the mid-60s, India and Pakistan's stick manufacturers were gleefully exporting the long English heads to the Motherland whilst their national teams were running rings around solid but limited British opponents at the Olympics with their tight, trimmed hockey sticks.

Arguably it was in this sector of stick shape evolution that the most marked dynamic occurred during these decades of Asian supremacy. For years importing nations were insistent on the English heads, and what informed commentators could not understand was why European players and coaches could not see the advantages for more diverse manoeuvres with the stick, notably in individualised drag movements of the ball. It was like in football, two competing teams, one side was all one footed against a team that had mastered two footed play….. The result was no contest.

Eventually technology did overtake this situation as European innovators brought stiffened reinforced fibre hockey sticks to the market by the early 80's which not only improved aerial and power passes, but coincided with the declining prowess of the Asian teams in International competition. As noted, Britain's Commonwealth provided a great launching pad for these Indian teams during these mid-century decades. Tours were commonplace to Hong Kong, Singapore, Malaysia, Australia, New Zealand, Uganda, and Kenya. Significantly, it could be claimed that these Indian teams both pre- and post-partition in 1947, were the equivalent to the Harlem Globetrotters Basketball exhibitions in the USA in the second half of the century. They were almost exhibition matches, non-contests as competitive matches, but what they did achieve was the carriage of hockey quality to two new continents, Africa and Australasia.

Test matches were played in all the big cities stretching from Nairobi to Perth, Sydney, and Christchurch. Naturally, crowds flocked to see Dhyan Chand and the Unbeatables. Yet, more poignantly, these hockey visits had left many disciples in their wake, sprouting an increased enthusiasm for hockey, and how the game could prosper in those countries lucky enough to have witnessed the structure, the technical skills, and the attacking emphasis of the Indian style of play. This was nowhere better illustrated than on the famous India tour of Australia and New Zealand of 1935. New Zealand and Western Australia still today are full of references to the images and influences that were dispersed during that one tour of 48 matches when over 500 goals were scored.

Disciples of the Indian style were numerous, but one who dedicated his life to the teaching and coaching in that mould was New Zealander Cyril Walter. He was an outstanding International player in his own right, but Cyril has become known as one of the true practitioners of hockey coaching in the Twentieth Century. His books and daily practice reinforced the timelessness of coaching individual skills on the sports field. In a coaching career that spanned four decades he was deeply committed to hockey in his home town of Christchurch and his Canterbury University base as he extolled the lessons he had learned from that 1935 tour.

As time progressed, many of those Indian players who had toured the Empire had opportunities to settle in those far-flung lands that had been open and willing to enthuse over their hockey. Families literally emigrated to Perth, Kampala, or Singapore for a new life, many of whom had been posted to those nations to work in the Railways or the Military and subsequently had stayed. Indian migration was very commonplace after partition, and in hockey terms, this development had a profound effect upon the sport's growth, notably in East Africa and in South-East Asia.

4

Between 1947 and 1972, just a quarter of a century, hockey's dynamic was clear to see where in Kenya and Uganda by the later date the two African nations were ranked in the top ten of the world. The very first World Cup in Spain in 1971 resulted in Pakistan and Kenya in the semi-finals, Asia and Africa ; not really, it was all Asia.

Just one year later, the Ugandan National Squad was announced in Kampala to play in the Olympic Tournament at Munich, and it included Rajinder Singh Sandhu as the stylish centre-half and captain of Uganda at the zenith of their powers. Jinder's family was steeped in hockey with his father very much involved in playing and managing in his original home province of the Punjab in India.

After partition in 1947, the farm was not providing a worthwhile source of income, so the family uprooted to take a job on the Railways expansion in East Africa. Prior to this event, his father was rejected by the British Army as a result of sporting a very healthy beard at the age of 17. The military just did not believe he was that young!

Jinder's progress as a promising player was typical of his generation of Indian migrants to Uganda, Kenya and Tanzanir. They had the facilities to play the game at government schools and the clubs afforded a strict adherence to ethnic identity with separate fields and clubhouses for Sikhs, Goans, Moslems and the colonial power's dominant British base in more lavish surroundings.

This division at the time was seen as quite natural with the lack of interest for hockey and cricket amongst the indigenous Ugandan population. There were 35,000 Asians in the country by the mid 60's, but interestingly that total comprised regional Indians that really had made a specific contribution to set sectors of professional life in their newfound home. Goans, particularly well organised, held posts in the Civil Service, the Sikhs occupied positions in the Railways and Utilities with the Moslems who worked in Public Buildings. The native born Ugandans were more attracted to life in the Military or the Police Force, notably after their Independence from Britain in 1963.

Education, the schools and colleges, was another area in which the Indians held great influence. The teacher vocation was dominated by migrants from the sub-continent, but this never really extended to the art of coaching hockey. Jinder offered this point:

"In our school days, we were supplied with Indian hockey sticks. The Indian Maharaja was the best, and we were just allowed to run free. No single person taught us the skills. We used to play cricket and hockey at the same time, playing school matches and attending tournaments at centres like Jinja, but we picked up the most by watching the adults compete at weekends and by being exposed to touring Indian or Pakistani teams that included Kampala as a match venue. Also, the annual test matches against Kenya and Tanzanir were always eagerly anticipated."

Essentially, all this did not matter as hockey was in their blood. It was work, religion, family and hockey, but in an outdoor paradise, not necessarily in that order!! Word soon spread to India via relatives and the British Mail system and the relaxed migration procedures encouraged by the Brits did allow more workers to join their extended families in Nairobi and Kampala from India. Hockey therefore grew, and soon, an annual quadrangular was introduced between the colonial Brits, the Goans, the Indians and the host Africans. Jinder remembered this round robin event fondly:

"There was a great deal of rivalry, and the tournament aroused huge emotions, mainly between the Goans and the Indians who included a mix of Hindus, Sikhs and Moslems. The British were an inconsistent team depending on which players were available from the military units, whilst the Africans still were mastering a relatively new game for them. The final was often contested between the Indians and their off-shore island of Goa."

Uganda's Olympic Squad would have been drawn from these groupings and it produced the mercurial talent of Kuldip Singh Bhogal, soon to be voted the most outstanding individual player at the Munich Games. The author of these papers as a young County player spent an afternoon at Abbeydale Sports Club in Sheffield attempting to keep him under wraps later in 1972. He was playing for Yorkshire, of all teams. They had never seen his like before. His change of direction at pace with the ball still firmly on the stick was truly amazing. My County Durham team lost 0-1, but we never knew to this day how we kept it to a one goal deficit.

Kuldip was finished with Uganda. Just imagine if you are able to, you are selected to go to an Olympiad as Africa's second seeded team in June, then simultaneously the tyrant Idi Amin gives the same players ninety days to leave the country. How could a squad perform to anywhere near the best of their abilities under such stress? Uganda ranked in the top 10, bombed to 15th place after a succession of narrow defeats, even just by one goal to eventual gold medalists West Germany. Everything, employment, family, sport, house, social life had to be terminated during this same period. When Rajinder and Kuldip left Kampala for Munich, they were only to return to pick up their life belongings, before heading into the great unknown.

Hockey was destroyed, and Uganda was never to reappear on the world stage again. Yes, it all happened in 1972. Their neighbours Kenya for that moment were left alone to carry hockey forward in East Africa.

Kenya, having gained a semi-final place at the inaugural World Cup in '71, lost out in Munich to the new levels of mobility, strength and tactical awareness of the European nations. Maybe they too were destabilised by Uganda's fate as they faced African freedom movements in their own country and they feared the worst for their own future.

The colonial power, Britain, took in the fleeing Asians, and encouraged by this, many Kenyan Indians looked to the mother country as a focal point for educational opportunities. Hockey-wise, a lenient three year residency qualification guaranteed an England future for younger players like Sutinder Khehar and Balwant Singh Saini. The older players like Kuldip cut their losses and looked to a professional future away from hockey in Canada, the U.S.A, or Britain. Those that came to England fell into the welcoming arms of Jimmy James who was the manager of "the London Indians" club invitation team. How those estranged players from India and East Africa loved that benevolent hockey character. He was like a father to each and every one of them.

London Indians produced fantastic opposition to a succession of England teams preparing for major tournaments as they represented the style and quality of all the Asian teams of that period. The club would itself contribute double figure players, indoors and out, and future Olympic medalists for England and Great Britain. Some of the club's players shuttled to and from Kenya for internationals, but the game there dissipated with no government investment in hockey, only into the cause of the popular and successful distance running. The country was to play its last Olympic tournament in 1984, even more deeply scarred by emigration and a lack of facilities and internal competition. It was never to be the same as in the years after partition.

Indeed the tragedy of Ugandan hockey really was a political one, but what about back home in India during these dramatic years as European nations, for the first time, were winning World Cups and Olympics?

Were there, therefore, any real internal reasons for demise? It must be noted that decline was gradual at first with India still winning the World Cup in 1975 in an all-Asian final, but as the Montreal Olympics and the Argentina World Cup suggested, suddenly the names of Holland, Australia and New Zealand were occupying the final placing. Pakistan, in particular, produced a golden generation with Aktar Rasool, Manzoor Junior, and Samiullah Khan prominent, but India were not to gain a single Olympic or World Cup medal from that day in 1975 until today (*The boycotted Games of 1980 are not included).

Let us investigate India more closely, but first take note that Pakistan's curve of decline was not really noticeable until arguably ten or fifteen years later. The country was a more closed entity in terms of culture, religion, and diversity. For sure, the golden generation which was to win two World Cups and one Olympic title between 1978 and 1984, as in Dhyan Chand's era, led to further role model quality as the next generation of Shahbaz Ahmad and Tahir Zaman followed suit briefly in the early 90s.

India's society was more modern, and open to the processes of globalisation that ran like wildfire through the world after 1980. Such a world was becoming smaller with large scale emigration to Britain, the USA, Canada, Australia, the Far East, and Europe. The actual numbers in quantity were insignificant in relation to the massed millions back home but many of these emigrants were in the educated sector where hockey people had tended to congregate in the professional field of employment.

Secondly, India was still beset with regional bias and polarisation. As early as 1977 it was not unusual to witness at International matches based at the Nehru Tournament in Delhi where India would play England or Spain, and the home crowd of over 20,000 would have screamed in favour of the touring European team. Why such an outrage? The answer lay in the composition of that India National Team which might have been full of southern Indians rather than the Sikh dominated northern players of the Punjab.

Clearly this was an interdenominational concern and something which crossed the frontiers of hockey with overall life. Temples had been stormed, periodic riots and tensions in set regions all contributed towards mutual suspicion and rivalry. India was made up of Hindus, Sikhs, Muslims, Christians, and a host of minority faiths. Cultural beliefs that the game of Dhyan Chand belonged in the heartland of the Punjab were undermined whilst the Indian authorities were selecting players, coaches, and managers from the big cities down south like Bombay, Madras, and

Calcutta. Inevitably, these regional anxieties have occurred in all big nations in hockey, but India had always the problem of distances between centres that had only been linked by very slow means of rail transport, and a virtual non-existence of fast, effective highways.

Thus, coaching and developmental ideas were locked into certain parts of the country often over 1000 miles apart, and misunderstandings on issues were easily formulated or deliberately exploited. The term 'Team India' has seldom been heard since 1975, and whereas in the halcyon years of hockey when the national tournaments brought the diverse areas together, today they often just have accentuated the differences. Coaching, in particular, has been singularly lacking not only in terms of the national teams, but also in the implementation of common core coaching ideals across the country at organised youth level and in encouraging the participation of young women to the sport.

Australia and Canada, as big countries, soon took up the initiative to take measures to ensure that all the states were singing off similar hymn sheets. In India too much stress was placed on the selection procedures to teams rather than an evolutionary approach to developing young players through the age groups up to senior levels. Evidence of this is highlighted from the Junior U-21 World Cup statistics since 1978 where India has participated in all ten tournaments.

Probably in FIH terms the most successful Senior International team has been Germany over the modern period covered in these papers. Relevant to this is their concentration on the merits of their Under-21 squad in major Junior World Cups. Germany, more than any other nation, has understood the correlation between these two levels, their Under 21 teams have won a resounding six gold medals from the ten tournaments.

India has only achieved one and so has Pakistan in 35 years, a 20% success rate for Asian hockey, far removed from pre-1972 levels.

With huge human potential, the success progressively since the Junior World Cup was inaugurated, had been noticeably meagre, and if only numbers of hockey participants under the age of 21 were available, it would surely show an ever decreasing decline in numbers in the decades since 1980. We have a chicken and egg scenario here. Did the numbers decrease because of India's demise since that date as a potent world force? Or did the under-population of hockey enthusiasts lead to a terminal drop in performance?

There is one other easy answer, a small word called...............Cricket! The game which used to go hand in glove in all British colonial enclaves was now providing the nails into the proverbial Indian Hockey coffin. The sporting balance of hockey played in the cooler, wetter months and then cricket focused on the hotter summer months was consistent wherever you looked in the Commonwealth nations. Here in India, young boys pre-1972 were equally adept at the two disciplines, and often found it difficult to choose which one to follow.

Now cricket was offering two games in the form of one sport: The Test Match, and The One Day Game. It was no accident that after the introduction of Kerry Packer's cricket circus in 1977 and its inevitable televising of this one day game with exciting new rules, coloured clothing and balls, and the financial rewards that came along with this new phenomenon, that all of India would be converted to the new Cricket very readily.

The only sport where there had been collateral damage had been to the game of hockey in India. As the decades unfolded and India's major cities, already endowed with major Cricket Test Match stadiums, prompted the India Cricket Board to take advantage of TV rights, advertising, and coverage to hungry audiences in England, South Africa, Australia, Sri Lanka, and New Zealand. Cricket had modernised much more readily and rapidly than hockey, taking an enterprising view on the involvement of such vital generous sponsors like Sahara. The latter was more than just a money provider; it basically had introduced an appealing and successful spectator product for the young.

It also set the background to improving the quality of the play both on and off the field. On the field it was noticeable that whereas India had produced a succession of capable International batsmen, they were relatively light in the tradition of rearing a stable of pacey, fast bowlers. Kapil Dev aside, there were few such match winners for India in the Twentieth Century. How was this remedied?

With the assistance of the sponsors, Dennis Lillee,the Australian guru of fast bowling technique, was unashamedly approached to support India's cause by personalised professional involvement. In other words, India Cricket from an early stage, yes, not lacking in resources, was never shy to ask for International help to areas of weakness. This simply was not the case in hockey until deep into this twenty-first century.

It could well be argued, as is the case in subsequent chapters, that it was too little too late for coaching interventions in hockey in 2010. India had failed to recognise the seed of their alarming decay as a hockey force as early as 1980. Whereas India Cricket had received the jolt of Packer's Revolution, another event was also to send Indian Hockey authorities into reverse for over three decades, and it resulted from the winning of an Olympic gold medal in 1980!!

The 1980 Moscow Olympiad was definitely a total hockey farce as Czechoslovakia lined up against Zimbabwe, Cuba and Angola. It was the big boycott with no Argentina, Australia, Canada, Germany, Great Britain, Holland, Kenya, Malaysia, New Zealand, Pakistan, Belgium, or South Africa. India beat Spain 4-3 in a discredited final, and in the first Women's Hockey Olympics, Zimbabwe won the gold!! Rather than rue the day they participated in the tournament, India celebrated a hollow victory. The resultant complacency really did extend over three decades where the previous Invincibles could not even bring home a single hockey medal of any type.

It has been very easy for Indian Hockey followers to explain this all away, as they have, to an FIH conspiracy, to new rules, surfaces, training methods, etc. Yet these pages have revealed concrete reasons how they themselves could have controlled their own destiny to retain standards for the game in India.

Coaches have come and gone, as have managers, but what has remained the same throughout this period has been the reluctance to adapt both on and off the field. They always knew better, and what was incomprehensible was that they could see at first hand the early continuing success of Pakistan and their brand of Asian hockey. The Indians failed to see the inherent discipline in the Pakistan play and organisation, which had at least kept their northwestern neighbours at the top for at least another ten years until political instability in that country forced many of their sports teams into a nose dive after 1994.

The science of coaching had equally passed India by, as coach after coach could not come to terms with the successes of European and Australasian teams after 1985. Like all good coaches they had to be excellent thieves, not to copy the Aussies or the Dutch, but to extract by observation and analysis the elements of their game which India could revamp to their own advantage. Indeed, is not exactly that which Australia and New Zealand coaches and teachers had done having witnessed the great Indian teams of yesteryear?

Indian coaches seldom ventured overseas to observe, let alone coach in foreign environments. In fact, it has been a very short list of coaches in India in the last 30 years that have made any impact whatsoever with any of the National teams. Their knowledge had not contained enough breadth of experience, nor had it received any positive new initiative in approach to the sport. Tactical variations, indoor hockey, sports medicine, and video analysis had literally left India in their wake in the later years of the twentieth century. Newly adapted skills on AstroTurf came as a late shock to Indians when facing International players who presented them with new problems on the field of play.

Complacency followed the tragic event of the Moscow Olympics and it was not only India that was to falter. Note earlier its acolytes in Malaysia, Singapore, and East Africa had also plummeted in terms of International performance and in the popularity of the game itself. The very same followers, teachers, and enthusiasts had looked to India for solutions to their own decline, but they, in turn, were looking in the wrong direction. Malaysia seldom bothered the top ten in the world game again, with Kenya and Uganda blown off the hockey map and hardly ever even participating in International competition.

Indeed, as events unfolded into the twenty-first century and headed towards the World Cup of 2014 in the Netherlands, Pakistan had not even qualified whilst India pursued a revolving door of hiring overseas coaches to survive at this level. This short-term emphasis, in itself, reflected the desperation of the sub-continent as they belatedly looked for help after three decades of visible decline.

Their alternative plan to create a mixed multi – national league to be contested over a short period each year has attracted eager foreign players and coaches motivated by generous sponsors' financial backing. But has this development been in the interests of grass roots hockey for India? It was all too little too late, a sideshow that to date has neither stimulated national team success nor attracted a ground swell of spectators back to hockey.

The FIH simply have been reactive to the continent's demise. Not comprehending the economic transition of India's middle class in cities like Mumbai and Delhi, who now possess purchasing powers to have real choice to their leisure time, the International body has singularly ignored the claims of the provinces to host major events. The satellite cities in the Punjab, central India and Lucknow would have filled their stadia to stage a Junior World Cup or Champions Challenge. Capital cities demand success and Delhi's cricket fans have experienced that privilege, but have known that it had been missing from hockey for some time.

The real issue had passed India by through world hockey's reawakening in the late 70's and 80's when those in charge of the Indian Hockey Federation had refused to recognise a changing hockey world, where middle ranked nations like Korea, Argentina and New Zealand had overtaken, in most respects, both India and Pakistan, and in turn had produced world class women's squads as well. In those countries, the process of development of the game at all levels was paramount to their progress. India had never learned that harsh truth.

In a matter of less than fifteen years, the era of Asian dominance had come to an abrupt end. The internal strife that has been outlined in this chapter was surely the result of 'The Hockey Dynamic' that was to envelope the game and whisk it away from its traditional base of homeland Britain and its proudest former Jewel in the Crown, Imperial India. These twin pillars had set the scene for hockey in its early expansion and competitive days. Indeed before the Penalty Corner expertise of Michael Krause, it could be argued that there was little competition. The Asian Giants ruled the hockey world and had put one over their lorded masters from those sceptered islands off the coast of Europe.

The British, in turn, had their own problems with their hockey in a post-war world that was yielding huge social upheaval. With their propensity to benevolent organisation, the Brits had helped India to a level of predominance in the world game that they themselves could only dream of, but meanwhile in their own backyard, Hockey's establishment nation was to face their own infamous winds of change.

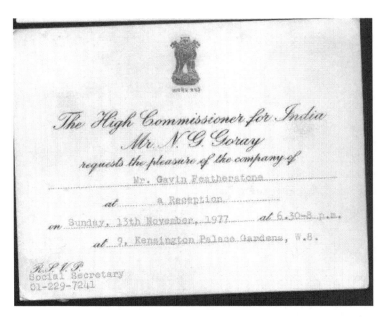

When England toured India, governments became involved!

"Storm Kills 879", but Hockey gets the headlines, India, 1977

When Asia ruled supreme ; Pakistan win the World Cup.

A warning shot from a young English coach in 1981

The Old Boys Network

Prime Minister Harold MacMillan, of course, was referring to social and political evolution in Africa and India and beyond in his 1960 Winds of Change speech. Many who lived through that post- war period knew that Britain not only as a colonial power had to yield to the independence demands of its Commonwealth, but also to the voices from within.

Youth culture had invaded British society in fashion, art, music and sport. The country had introduced so much to the world and now by the 60's it was time for the Brits to take a look at themselves and fathom out a new role for the future both on and off the playing fields.

Over the previous century, the structured game of hockey for men and women had been introduced into the schools and clubs as a sporting way of life across the country. Hockey's organised origins in the latter half of the nineteenth century were soon to be transplanted from the southern counties of England to Argentina, Canada and the United States, to Australia and New Zealand, to Kenya, Rhodesia, Uganda and South Africa, to all parts of Europe, and as we have seen to Malaya and the Indian sub-continent.

The British had secured a major foothold in the sport's structure, rules, administration and play, even introducing hockey as an Olympic sport in the first decade of the new century. Yet, its stranglehold was loose as there were no major events to bind hockey together like international tournaments or World Cups. This fragmentation along with the First World War dissolved any overall control until the French formalised the game as an Olympic sport for the 1928 Olympics. Britain's jewel in the crown, its right hand man, India, was to take over on the field both the competitive and missionary edge of the sport right through to 1972.

Back inside Britain by 1964, the Labour Party took political control, and broader educational policies took hold as the former rigid tripartite schools system of Public Schools (private), Grammar Schools and Secondary Moderns was to be dismantled by government decree. Rigid selection at the age of eleven was regarded as divisive and in most counties the more academic Grammars were disbanded, giving way to Comprehensive Schools.

Most commentators would regard the heading of "The Old Boys Network" as to refer to that small but deeply rooted public schools system which educated less than 7% of the population. However, the real battle was not at that level because the Grammars were the target for the government. To the Labour faithful, they stood for selection, discipline and competition, qualities not high on the government's agenda. They freely presented the opportunities for young boys and girls to climb the social and economic ladder of life, and this was reflected in the number of their pupils gaining places at top Universities.

What was all this to do with hockey? The Grammars were centres for youth hockey, for boys and girls. Their teachers were often trained at academic Universities where they themselves had played in University clubs. There was a learning and dedicated environment within these schools that had produced countless club, representative and international players over the previous half century. The names of Beckenham and Kingston Grammars acted as prominent nurseries for future Olympians. That was until they faced successive governments that threatened their existence.

The trouble was that the Comprehensive schools basically took on the mantle in sports education of the previous Secondary Moderns. They generally inherited the premises, essentially just renaming them. It was definitely a stated aim to give a comprehensive education by broadening the curriculum, both academic and sporting. This inevitably did not occur as the great majority of these new idealised schools took on a populist stance by only offering boys football and occasionally rugby as winter sports. They had, essentially, locked out hockey for boys.

Those that did offer hockey were also subjected to other state decrees of discouraging competition between schools in team sports. The much advertised Sports Council doctrine of "Sport for All" was meant to push leisure and recreation in physical activity, not competition and achievement. Heads of Schools, often clones to government guidelines just sidelined sport into the demesne of the local hockey clubs at this stage who could offer nothing in the way of teaching the game with precious little resources or coaching expertise.

So, with a scarcity of school matches and a diminution of active hockey teachers, notably males, apathy was the order of the day and starting in the late 60's it was that way for decades to come. English hockey now had to rely on the exclusive private schools for its quality recruits, but within that system, there were two big drawbacks.

Firstly, they only played for ten weeks in the year, the worst ten in terms of dreadful weather from January to March. In many of these boarding schools, hockey players were treated like second class citizens by their peers and regrettably by the physical education staff itself. Hockey acted as an interim measure between the major outlets for prestige, rugby played in the temperate autumn and cricket in the warmer summer months.

Secondly, the public school system was there to prepare the pupils for the professions: law, medicine, finance, the City and up until then the diplomatic corps and Empire. The youngsters educated at these prestigious establishments would recreate with hockey with a high fun component, but seldom did they engender the kind of competitive environment that had shaped Dhyan Chand, Luciana Aymar or Ric Charlesworth.

These battles would rage on as more and more Grammars were shut down with the old school tie a sentiment from history. The situation deteriorated as some whole counties decided to support, in defiance, direct grant schools and joined the Independent sector. In hockey terms, the game was losing out on numbers participating, but, at least those that were educated throughout the 70's in Grammars contributed seven of the gold Olympic Final team of 1988. This was a clear testament to the values that Chatham House had given to Sean Kerly, Sir William Borlase to Jon Potter, and that Kingston G.S. had supplied to Richard Dodds.

They were the lucky ones, because their schools had survived the takeovers. To every one Sean Kerly, there were ten boys denied the chance to play hockey at school. English hockey in the 80's had needed the boost that future comprehensive education would recognise the fact that hockey was a boy's and man's sport. That undertaking never materialised. It was to have a major impact on participation and national team achievement in the decades either side of the millennium as Olympic and world results slid into mediocrity.

Nevertheless, the Old Boys network was alive and kicking in the British Commonwealth of nations. Britain had spread a whole range of modern cultural, commercial and infrastructural development across the world, but none more so than in education. Naturally all these nations had experimented and expanded with the base provided by prominent philanthropists and educators whether in the American college system, the Kenyan Preparatory schools or the state Grammar or High schools in Australasia and South Africa.

It was noticeable that the southern hemisphere prospered from these schools because they yielded a more formal education that early state governments strongly supported. A steady stream of top sports personalities emerged from Auckland and Sydney Grammar Schools as competition between schools drove up standards in the classroom and on the games fields.

In Johannesburg to this day, on any given Saturday morning, you will see hundreds to low thousands lined up along the touch lines to watch King Edwards School (KES) play Parktown Boys. Up continent it was always the same in the boarding and day prep school system around Nairobi in Kenya as boys and girls that thrived in sport at the age of ten or twelve would have the potential not only to play top adult sport, but also to take responsible positions of leadership in life.

Wherever there has been British influence, from Buenos Aires to Christchurch, Singapore to Jamaica, Vancouver to Madras, a tight network of rival schools with an inbuilt competitive framework has been the impetus for the growth of team sport and had equally formed the bedrock for national and international success in hockey.

All these nations saw no need to change, emphatically not when it came to physical education. A case study would be in hockey at the very central school of Jeppe Quondam in Johannesburg. The school retained very high academic standards and offered a thorough education to diverse communities adjoining the high rise blocks of the inner city. The school's playing fields were two miles away and the kids were bussed out to learn their hockey three times a week after school in the afternoons with intense games against rival schools at weekends.

On South Africa's reintroduction to international hockey at the World Cup in 1994, with government insistence on all inclusive and fair selection, Jeppe provided five old boys of the sixteen squad, Charles Pereira, Sean Cooke, Craig Jackson, Robbie Pullen and Brad Michalaro. This demonstrated the continued value in States investing in this more formalised system of education with firm ground rules allowing students to broaden their impact at school as they physically and emotionally matured.

In strict contrast, the British old boys and girls network had been sorely challenged by political and then educational agendas in these latter decades of the twentieth century. It was damaged but not eliminated. It survived as the traditions of sporting prowess aligned with academic success meant that these twin towers of education had been passed on together to the tertiary sector, the Universities and Colleges.

University sports clubs were a feature of life for students who had moved on from schools to seek the opportunity to play hockey as a means to create a social and a professional life at college and beyond their university years. Indeed, University cultural life, in academic, political and social interest societies could achieve the same end, but not quite as effectively as the bonds that were formed within team sporting structures.

The connection for instance between an Oxford College like Balliol with high office in government (the college boasted three ex British Prime Ministers in its history) was commonplace as colleges assumed high reputations in specific fields of academia and life skills that would intrinsically link them with certain professions. Nowhere was this more marked than in sport and hockey in particular. The preponderance of Oxbridge international players for England no doubt peeked in the colonial heydays from 1930 -1970. Our table inset depicts how the influence of the Oxbridge network declined dramatically at World Cup selection level in the twenty years from the European Cup in 1970.

ENGLAND SELECTED PLAYERS FROM OXBRIDGE EDUCATIONAL ORIGIN AT WORLD CUP LEVEL	
SQUAD TOTAL -- 16	
1973	FIVE
1978	THREE
1982	TWO
1986	ONE
1990	NIL

During this period individual private schools and a minority of emerging grammars had constructed direct links between their academic departments and specific colleges at Oxford and Cambridge. Former University scholars that had climbed the educational pole to become Headmasters clearly placed a great deal of emphasis on the number of their pupils who could follow in their footsteps.

In the author's experience of playing in the senior hockey team at Kingston Grammar School, four of the team had applied to Cambridge colleges in 1969 and had instant success. There was no question of applying to

Oxford or any other prevalent institution, because Percy Rundle as the Headmaster was a distinguished Master of Arts at Cambridge. It was as simple and as contrived as that!!

Interestingly, two of the four became full internationals, pre-empting a tide of Kingston boys in the 70's connected to St. Catherine's College culminating in future Olympic Gold medal captain Richard Dodds O.B.E. Cambridge had established many such conveyor belts of sporting talent both from schools and in the postgraduate sector as graduates descended on to further study.

One of English hockey's such rising stars in 1972 was a true son of this conveyor belt of public schoolboys into the hallowed halls of the Cambridge colleges. Graeme Menzies was a stylish zonal full back, educated at the four hundred year old boarding school in Essex called Felsted. Coached by the great Corinthian triple blue and Olympian from 1952, John Cockett, Graeme followed a long line of England and Great Britain players produced in this hotbed of a hockey nursery. Cockett was a masterly centre-half himself and had schooled for that year's Munich Games two of Britain's most outstanding core players in Richard Oliver and Tony "the Ox" Ekins.

Yet, unlike Oliver, who had entered Oxford in the mid – sixties, Graeme was now exposed to a world of change in hockey where training was expected to double or triple the time spent on the match field. It was a hockey world of new systems of tactical play, of sweepers, man to man markers and fluid strikers. Indeed Cockett's secure base of swivelling full backs, commanding centre halves and, from the line wide wingers, was becoming old hat.

Graeme also had to face serious positional competition from a new breed of boys educated outside of the comfortable public school sector. His move to Cambridge did not, in this respect, help him either as a festive old boys culture of 'train hard, drink hard', was to envelop Cambridge Blues teams for years to come.

Was this really surprising when a good Cambridge degree in the professions would set up any of these players in an England on full employment? Surely with hockey offering no financial recompense and no career prospects, this was all a no- brainer!! The evidence was there for all to see as the decade leading up to 1973 had yielded over 10 Cambridge blues promoted to the England and Great Britain teams, only one succeeded in securing such a regular place between 1973 and 1983.

So I asked Graeme what had happened to affect such a change:

"We were aware that academic pressure was becoming tighter at this time as Cambridge really was assuming a more scientific base with new laboratories sprouting up in building form for medicine and engineering. This meant that more committed time in the afternoons was expected of the students, and this factor seemed to create a different balance to the make-up of the students compared to the past."

Whereas Cambridge was changing its academic emphasis in the classroom with its eleven Blues from 74 made up of three future University lecturers, three School teaching heads of departments, two doctors and three lawyers, the hockey dynamic was non-existent. Graeme remembers:

"There really was no senior guidance or coaching, the captains did everything. In essence we played three matches a week, and in between times, all I can remember was hours working on fitness runs, circuit training and penalty corners. There were times with additional Essex County training that I would return to College near to midnight and be physically sick, we were so fit. Even though I was selected for the England U21 Squad, I never felt through Cambridge that I was getting better technically.

I was four years a Law Student and even though hockey had been thoroughly enjoyable, there was no doubt in my mind that Law School was beckoning me after Cambridge with the requirements of the inevitable Articles which I would take up in a London Practice. I wanted to continue with my hockey, but I had come to realise that the rest of the 70's was to be a matter of getting fully qualified and in my case, to start a family.

At the instigation of one of my more festive Cambridge friends, I believe an old schoolmate of yours, Gav, I joined a very sociable club, Surbiton, at the recommendation of Clive Hicks. In those days playing in the London League with a club that lacked ambition in their performance meant that you could develop your networking skills in the professional world as there were numerous colleagues as contemporaries that I have kept up with right through to today."

Graeme took up a career move to Hong Kong in '78, before returning several years later in accepting to run a small but emerging Law Firm in Norfolk in the early 80's. By then, he had long surrendered any hopes or aspirations of achieving any honours on the hockey field. That small Norfolk firm now in 2014 employs hundreds of employees in the UK and

North America, including one Graeme Menzies as the Senior Partner based, where else, than in the centre of his beloved Cambridge. Mills and Reeve has been kind to Graeme, who in his sixtieth year, was to leave our meeting in his luxurious office on the sixth floor for an urgent appointment. He was to play for an East of England Over 60's Veteran team at the World Cup in Holland!! Ever the smooth full back that the author used to partner in the days of England Under 21 and Ziggy Stardust!!

Graeme's story replicates so many talented British young players that really were not given much of a choice right through to the end of the century whether to forego a professional career for the sport they loved so much. Yet, through hockey, they would all admit that they would build a tremendous network of friends and acquaintances that would complement their success as their careers unfolded.

It was not just the Old Boys that worked at the network. As the sport developed in the nineteenth century and Empire had spread across the continents, colonial men did not regard the rough and ready version of the game as suitable for women. It was considered too dangerous and they believed that women had more important roles in nurturing families in industrial England and in the challenging environments of the colonies. This notion was soon to be contested as younger students rallied and the first club hockey was introduced in the 1880's for female players in the London suburbs, over thirty years before women got the vote!!

Such a young enthusiast was Constance Applebee, who had left her Essex home early in the new century to venture to America where she was the original pioneer of the game there, a true educationalist and feminist who was to lay the foundations of field hockey for American colleges like Harvard. She achieved this by demonstrations, and by accepting physical education positions at Bryn Mawr College near Philadelphia.

This icon of the game followed similar paths to all the exponents of the sport in British colonies. She gave scant recognition to the reality that men had played the game for near on half a century and indeed, had invented the modern form of organised hockey. The strict adherence to female issues was just a part of her demeanour, exacerbating the potential divisions in the early growth of the game.

Her take on the sport was that it had to be focused around fun and friendship as an overview to attracting the social nature of females, but it was a fact, as any of her students would have testified, she was a harsh practitioner and overseer of coaching the game sternly. Her legacy was very deep-rooted as she lived into the twenty-first century, and this assured a succession of acolytes down through the generations to protect her philosophy on the game. Ask any High School player today to name a male player, or have they ever heard of Jamie Dwyer, and their answers will be no, no again, with an additional question of their own, "Do men play field hockey?" In fact, many boys who have wanted to play the game have had to have the imposed indignity of wearing a girl's kilt to participate in High School hockey.

Whereas it is fair to acknowledge that hockey evolved very well in Europe to provide a close co-existence between men and women, this was never really the case in North America. The Old Girls network sprung up rapidly in the United States as the exclusive Prep Schools with female only teachers and coaches would pass on their aspirants to Ivy League Universities and eventually to the umbrella body for collegiate sport, the NCAA.

Try looking up hockey on a modern day website at any American University. First of all you will be directed to "Women's Sports", then onto Field Hockey. For a considerable number of decades men have been locked out of field hockey because of these perceptions. Today, men occupy only 8% of all Head Coach appointments in Collegiate Women's Division 1 field hockey, and not even that in Divisions 2 and 3 and High Schools. Gender disparity has held back the sport in America where the National women's team has won two solitary bronze medals at FIH level in World Cups or Olympics in 35 years of competition. Tragically, the Old Girls network here has not been inclined to expand the sport into adulthood either. Over the years, small millions have been confined to playing the game at high school and college level only, sold on the philosophy that this was the ceiling of hockey attainment.

In short, in America, the sport was secondary to a range of other agendas, perpetuated by the Old Girls network's protection of the game. So many enthused players wanted to continue playing after graduating, but none of them seemed to have questioned why there had not been any opportunity to do so, as in the rest of the world. Did they not find that ridiculous in the land of the free?

Back in the birthplace of the networking system, there had soon developed the concept of "The Club", how the British loved that institution, after all, they invented it!! Originally, new members had to be introduced by a current member, proposed and seconded, and then a vote could take place on the candidate's suitability. The horrendous implication of bias, prejudice and snobbery was prevalent.

It had become clear cut, where eventually blue collar workers would have filed into football clubs whilst the white collar chaps ventured into the more affluent world of hockey and rugby clubs.

Note the often quoted line, "Football is a gentlemen's game played by hooligans, and Rugby is a hooligans game played by gentlemen", definitely reflected the division that had developed in British sport. In order to cut this corner and to ensure that clubs were receiving the right type of fellow, actual Old Boys, or in Scotland, former pupils, clubs were established. They originally used their former schools facilities, but as they expanded, they found their own premises and fields with the designated function of being a social centre for networking Old Boys.

Many a business liaison was set up in the clubhouse after a competitive game as much as today the focus might be on the greens of the golf course. Once a University student had graduated and a move to the big city was about to be made, the Old Boys hockey club offered stability, a base to begin the professional life with the added bonus of an environment of familiar faces.

This comfortable but inward looking stance was to be broken down eventually by the hockey dynamic about to be unleashed onto this lifestyle which had never been altered until the 1970's. Networking was as much generational as functional as many examples of Old Boys Sports clubs have maintained their status throughout the British Commonwealth. Even today half or more of Johannesburg's Premier hockey division are either Old Boys or University clubs, and that is after twenty years of the African National Congress as the government.

London and England in general over the decades following 1970 have certainly seen a shift away from these clubs to more enlightened mixed gender clubs which have offered greater playing and social opportunities. In today's English National League of forty clubs, there is only one Old Boys entity, the Old Loughtonians Hockey club. It is fair to say that the club has survived by opening up its membership to all comers including a successful women's section that certainly did not attend Loughton Grammar School for Boys!!

These trace elements kept undermining the establishment on a gradual level and they worked alongside the effects of broader working possibilities for men and particularly for women. University specialist courses were stealing highly qualified undergraduates from the bastions of Oxford and Cambridge, and these areas of study often needed an urban, big city location. The old adage that the Armed Services or a Cambridge degree would lead to a direct route into the international teams was after 1972 a statement of declining authenticity as broader life choices were being made available to a much more fluid and flexible people.

Huge government investment had been placed into the expansion of the Polytechnics and technical colleges to meet the demands of growth sectors in plastics, chemical and oil derivative industries. At the same time, Britain was increasing its labour force with significant numbers of new commonwealth immigrants. Many, as chapter 1 highlighted, were from East Africa and India who had excelled at the game of hockey in nations that had no real direct exposure to how the British worked the network at home in their own country. They required leisure time facilities, as the demands on clubs to open up and become aware that women had been sold short in terms of participation and competition for too long had become regular in number. Clubs now had to offer broad social facilities where women and children would feel comfortable and welcomed with restaurants and play areas for young children. Few clubs until that point in time had even considered the needs of young families within sports and leisure clubs.

There were just too many internal pressures that were nibbling away at the continuation of the old network clubs, but it was to take two huge external factors that would finally push them over the edge, and both really were timed at the end of the 1970's.

This latest and arguably the broadest threat to the stability of both Old Boys and Girls networks was to be delivered from on high. Hockey, until the challenge of 1979 had been administered by the men and women's umbrella body, the Federation of International Hockey, the FIH, but was also led by the IFWHA. These initials had the W letter, which represented women exclusively. Formed back in 1929, it stubbornly held separate competitions under its own administration, which had close ties to the British Commonwealth and the United States.

So, we at last had reached the era when men and women would join forces to attract a wider audience, greater competition and more appeal to potential sponsors. There was still a great deal of work to be done with trying to merge a single gender organisation into the twentieth century, in 1980. Women in the IFWHA were absorbed with the fear that "their game" would be engulfed by the overbearing male committee chauvinists. The irony was that just by their very presence within the FIH, the leading women could and would break down the smoky gentlemen's club cosiness of Old Europe.

Indeed, that had essentially already been achieved within the FIH as constituent nations like Spain, Holland, Argentina and Germany were offering much needed diversity and fresh ideas to the advancement of the game. Like football and rugby union, hockey needed a truly global World Cup. Away with the Women's Conferences that sounded awful and were out of touch with the modern world, now it was the time to become one, and facilitate the first Women's World Championships in Kuala Lumpur in 1983. The FIH, without deliberate intent, was closing the door on the old school tie!!

The old world was under attack from a new generation ready to expand the sport, no doubt, but it was not to be a human factor which would take the network under, but a technological one which would present severe economic problems for limited clubs to survive. The first hockey dynamic to shake all the game's foundations, literally, was initiated from the most unlikely town in deepest Georgia in the America South. The town of Dalton would indirectly challenge every Old Boys Club's financial and commercial stability. The new addition would change the way the game was played for good, necessitate sweeping changes in the rules and equipment right down to the soles of our feet.

If those schools and clubs in Old hockey bastions in Europe, if those inward looking American colleges and the international and Olympic champions from India and Pakistan could not cope with the reality they were about to face, they would all inevitably fall from grace and quickly!! If they could not pay the price in almighty dollars and adapt to its demands, they would be overtaken as hockey nations.

The hockey world was to face the truth that natural grass was no longer dependable enough, and that a new technology was upon us in 1975. "One small step onto Turf, one giant leap for hockey". AstroTurf had arrived.

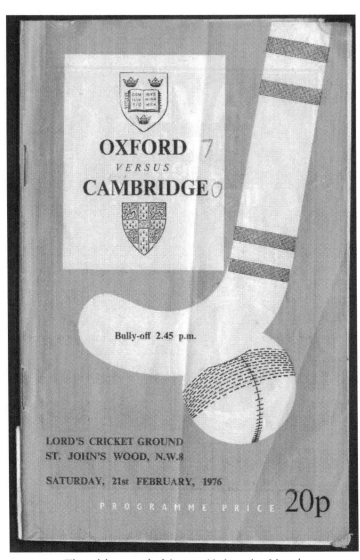

The oldest and ultimate University Match

Future professors, lawyers, doctors.. but no hockey Internationals;
Cambridge 1974

*The rewards for an Oxford Blue -
The Sweater and the Vincents Club tie !!*

The Folkestone International Hockey
Festival

request the pleasure of the company of

Captain, Old Athletic Palatinates H.C.

*at a Reception in honour of the Visiting Teams to be held at
Motel Burstin, Folkestone, on
Friday, 8th April, 1977*

Dress - Lounge Suits

8.30 - 10 p.m.

R.S.V.P.
MRS. N MIROY,
ELM LAWN,
LALEHAM-ON-THAMES,
MIDDLESEX TW18 2TD

PLEASE BRING THIS INVITATION WITH YOU

Hockey Festivals; A 4 day carnival of top Hockey and Inebriation!!

-Part C-
The AstroTurf Revolution

It started as a rumour from deepest Kuala Lumpur after the World Cup earlier in 1975. The Canadians, as hosts to the forthcoming Olympics a year later, were proposing to play the matches in one stadium on, of all things, artificial turf. The Asian world was not happy, seeing it as a western conspiracy to undermine their dominance of hockey in its competitive form. Even the Dutch and the Germans were quite shocked at such a transition as neither had invested in the dynamic polymer. Indeed, who had?

The answer to that one was the Americans. To hand, there was really just one company, Monsanto out of St. Louis, who had seen the need a decade earlier to experiment with synthetic fibre manufacture to provide sports facilities in any weather in any environment. Many American football games had been descending into farce and chaos as the northern winters took their toll on natural grass with deteriorating conditions as the season wore down the original grass fields.

Originally, fibre and weaving were no stranger to upstate New York and Massachusetts, but Monsanto wished to place this section of their industrial empire of carpet technology so that it was the core of the local economy with good access to ports for a business that could flourish in the export market. So, they upped sticks, as one could say, and moved their sports carpeting division to Dalton, Georgia.

The South knew a thing about cotton, wool and almost anything you could wear or stand on. More important than that was their ability to draw on the human expertise that accompanies these one industry towns, and Dalton already by the mid sixties boasted over one hundred and forty separate outlets for non-sporting carpet manufacture.

These were originally outlets, retail operations selling odd lots of carpet along the old US 41, between Atlanta and Chattanooga where an industry of sorts had evolved through craftswomen hanging their wares. The tufted carpet industry came out of the chenille industry, whilst the tufting innovation itself was credited to a couple of mountain women who persuaded the Singer sowing machine company into developing a sewing machine which could insert parallel rows of surface yarn into a canvas or other light backing material.

Here was a new process, new, uniform synthetic fibre yarns and cheap labour to feed the tufting machines for an expanding post-war American market. Fortunes were made in the Dalton hub.

The facilities were there and crying out for a group that would be searching for enough knitting and tufting machines to support the new sports market for surfacing of sports surfaces.

They also needed to attract the best human brains, specialists in chemical engineering that were prepared to research and develop products which were inevitably raw in the first place but would eventually come to dominate the world market in team sports over the coming half century. Such a brain was Ed Milner, who not only climbed the slippery pole from a synthetics engineer, through the products technology department to head the international marketing of AstroTurf, and finally take on the Presidency of AstroTurf in the late eighties. His was the most recognised rise of all, from shop floor through the test laboratories to the top of this global company in a world game.

Yet, the first sport it was to be introduced to was never to be a world game, just the most lucrative sport globally then and now -- it , of course was American football and the very first facility was to be the Houston Astrodome. The stadium was erected in 1966 and was to be the forerunner for many American and Canadian facilities for the ensuing decade.

One such stadium was the Empire stadium which hosted football and soccer with its early turtle backed shape to accommodate the winter drenchings of the British Columbia winters in Vancouver. Another minor team sport would appear there on Sunday mornings after the major sports competitions had died away from the Saturdays. It was Men's field hockey. Let Canadian Olympic team captain Alan Hobkirk take up the story:

"In Vancouver, we had been playing on artificial turf for several years at the old Empire Stadium(a North American football field). We had weekly Sunday four hour training sessions(7 a.m-11 a.m) with some premier league games played there. As planning for the 1976 Games was underway, it was readily apparent that, given the harsh winters and propensity for torrential rains during the summer, a grass surface would not be appropriate. At the time, the Canadian field hockey executive was based in Vancouver, and given what had been largely a positive experience from the players at the Empire with turf, the CFHA in conjunction with the Canadian Olympic Association and the FIH began to explore the use of artificial turf. All matches then could be played on one field at Molson Stadium which was another football facility at McGill University. The FIH yielded to these proposals on the understanding that the University host a pre-Olympic tournament in the summer of 1975."

Ed Milner was right at the centre of these deliberations from Monsanto's side as head of the products technology department. For several years with the ever increasing number of football stadia erected, he was dealing with issues of drainage, shock absorption for the players, UV degradation of the surface fibres, and the effects of traction on the players' ability to twist and turn at high speeds.

"We had some tremendous equipment to record ball speeds with frame per second technology as well as measuring the wear and tear on footwear. In American football we could note the difference in turning speed as the players cut against and with the directional fibre. This was purely an athletic and medical issue as there were early occurrences of ACL knee injuries. Little did we know then that once field hockey was introduced, we really had our work cut out on directional fibre(to you and me, the nap of the carpet)."

"However, we had the original AstroTurf product, and knitted nylon was the real thing with its hydrophilic properties, it merely absorbed the moisture within the fibre and held the water in the system for longer periods. We eagerly awaited the feedback from the '75 Pre-Olympic tournament to its true suitability for field hockey".

Alan Hobkirk was there leading the Canadian squad, and what a yarn he remembers to this day!!

"My first experience with the Astroturf was at the pre-Olympic tournament held in Montreal the summer of '75. A number of top hockey nations were invited to the tournament. Of course, many of these countries were playing on artificial turf for the first time, including Germany, Pakistan, Great Britain and Kenya. I do recall that the turf was watered with fire hoses, and, for some reason, early on, the watering appeared to be confined to the 100 yard by 60 yard playing surface and not the end zone or run off area."

"I remember that a German forward sprinted to the end of the pitch, reached the end zone, whereupon his foot slipped and planted onto the non-watered, high friction surface and he twisted his ankle. He went over and sustained a severe laceration to his thigh covering many square inches as a result of sliding on turf which was not appropriately watered. There were reports of the surface being so hot that the soles of playing shoes were melting. The Germans were furious and there was much talk about them going home."

"There was an evening game between Kenya and Mexico when the skies opened up and dumped at least an inch of water onto the field. It was covered with water and was unplayable for roughly ten minutes. There were the expected grumbles. However the skies cleared, the water quickly drained away, and the match resumed in perfect field conditions. I thought then that this was the turning point, when both players and organisers realised that this would be a very useful surface for tournament conditions (i.e. a very good surface that would not get chewed up with relatively uniform playing conditions from game to game throughout the tournament.) It was played in hot, humid conditions, and inevitably there were complaints about how hot it was in the 2 to 3 feet above the surface, no doubt due to the water evaporation."

"As the tournament progressed, nearly all involved thought that AstroTurf had the potential to revolutionise the game. The grumbling diminished with the final played between Pakistan and Germany, the score, 4-2 or 4-3 to Germany. It was a wonderful exhibition of hockey and augured well for the future of the game on Turf. Although I was not personally consulted in any specific way about the turf, the Canadian players thought it was the only logical choice for Montreal."

"At the Olympics themselves, the reaction was positive. I do not recall any negative comments about the field conditions (although India was certainly using it as an excuse for its poor performances). The stadium setting itself was quite magnificent with large crowds, which contributed to an excellent atmosphere."

So the ball was finally rolling on this dark green distinctive nylon carpet, and the FIH, under its autonomous President, Renee Frank, had a great deal to think about in the months that followed the Montreal Olympiad. First of all, was the ball rolling to everyone's satisfaction? Then there was the perennial problem of water, more water and how much water would be required for top tournaments? It was not long before Denys Cooper, as Secretary of the Canadian Association would write to AstroTurf's nylon carpet guru Ed Milner to address these two major drawbacks in the implementation of artificial surfaces for hockey. His concerns were clearly evident:

"As you will see by my final comment, my enthusiasm for the surface is apparent. It is nonetheless disturbing to see the effect that the nap of the turf(north to south) is having on a key element of the game, namely the penalty corner. It forced teams to take their penalty corners from the side WITH the nap, in preference to the natural position to the right of the goalkeeper. I was concerned when all the corners were added up that perhaps there was an aberration in the data, but by averages, there should be the same number of penalty corners at each end (split evenly for the 151 studied) - but the number of goals was different!"

Then, on water:

"Watering has to be a major area for further investigation as it affects the ball and the run of it. How resilient is the turf to having a watering truck pass over the field and spray the field - this would be more even than the hosing technique used in 1975. As your photos showed, the patchwork effect is definitely undesirable. Suitable rates of application would be required in the time available at half-time (5-8 minutes)."

Ed listened carefully, as he always did to personnel close to the sport. His was not a sporting background, but he knew a thing or two about problem solving. In short, he had to provide a non-directional pile for the punters! There were the demands from American football for consistent underfoot traction for those heavy set athletes to cut, and cut again at their leisure. Then there were the global inquiries, including from the author of these papers as a young international, of why did the hockey ball swerve to the outside of the pitch from a direct ball hit down the field? More, why did ball behaviour change across the pitch when you changed ends at half-time from smooth to choppy interaction with the surface? Then again, hockey on Turf had become a blood sport as any fall resulted in terrifying burns and scrapes in non- damp areas.

The Hockey Dynamic was set to work, and most of the answers were out there from the laboratories in Dalton before the end of the decade. The process of texturisation of the fibres was pushed forward very quickly and studies made into the hydrophilic properties of knitted and tufted nylon produced a softer feel to the grass which had once been described as a green brillo pad !!(an abrasive scouring brush for obstinate pots and pans) Even more than this, was the discovery from new forms of foam underlie that an Astroturf carpet could show great benefits from having a specialised layer of shock pad below the carpet.

What was it like to play in the five year transition period between grass and artificial turf? It was confusing as preparations varied from championship to championship. There seemed to be an early benefit to attacking teams like Pakistan, Holland and Australia as the more core defensive national units struggled to adapt to the faster pace and irregularities of the initial layered systems of turf. Certainly this was reflected in the late seventies and early eighties scorelines. There were a lot more goals. There were a lot more goals because there were a lot more skills on view! Players could now always use lateral ball transfer as an individual, and reap the benefits of easier one touch passes and deflections. Equally the power players could make the surface work for them by its reliability of faster movement for passes across the pitch. Defenders knew on the early surfaces that there was no way back from a failed committed tackle to retrieve the ball as the push off in turning was going to be an acquired art, placing more emphasis on stride pattern and lower weight transfer.

Of course there were some adaptations for attackers as well. They were to lose the lovely absorbent bounce from the aerial pass on grass for the forward chasers, and midfield players would need to possess that extra feel or touch in the through pass, but ,in general, it was open fast hockey that benefited most from the first generation of Astroturf. By 1980, AstroTurf as a product from Monsanto was king. Ed Milner, through his mastery of pile tilt angle, was looking forward into the realms of international marketing as he had nurtured a willing group of in-house engineers ever ready for the next improvement to their range of nylons. The group had a quality product base which players loved to perform on, so it cost more!!

Americans could afford it with a regeneration of the spending dollar in the 80's. From Dalton there was increasing supplies and expanding demand from American football franchises and a world interest from a wide array of hockey clients. The new Aussie hockey academies would buy into it throughout their states as did the Spaniards,the British and the Malaysians. Those doyens of Asian supremacy, India and Pakistan, moved very slowly with only 7 and 3 surfaces installed in the decade (contrast this to the city of Berlin where, alone, twenty seven combined hockey and soccer surfaces were there for continued use in the 80's).

The Europeans did not stand still. The sleeping carpet belt running from southern Holland through Belgium into northern France was to dramatically wake up after 1982 (note,after the FIH'S formal recognition of AstroTurf as a hockey leader). The second half of the game now was to show its hand as Europe looked across the Atlantic as if to say,"Now the real battle for Synthetic Turf Hockey begins!!!"

It was all a matter of cost and technology. The Netherlands was built from the low lying estuaries of Europe's great rivers, the Rhine and the Meuse. Much of the country was susceptible to flooding with many human tragedies, as recent as 1953 when more than 2,000 people lost their lives.

Sand and reclamation were the twin, hand in glove, responses to the Dutch problem of an expanding population in a dwindling small land area. Ironically, it was to be this national engineering base on sand technology that was to give the hockey community many more options for their playing and training potential both in hockey and football.

New companies or wings of huge chemical and textile magnates were to spring up in the 1980's to make Desso and Edel Grass, along with the fibre giant, Ten Cate, household names in pitch building for decades to come. They progressively entered the sports facilities market at just the right time as hockey was expanding its world base in the early part of "the synthetics decade".

Desso kicked it all off from their base in Oss, concentrating on a sand filled polypropylene product which was marketed across Europe at approximately less than half the price of a water filled AstroTurf. The early takers on the latter in Europe had been National Associations with budgets to spare. What about the local hockey clubs and schools? They were being priced out of the market, so it was this large sector of regular club or further educational entities that were most interested in the sand revolution.

The Matchmaker carpet was Desso's early flagship, often described by the AstroTurf giant as cheap and cheerful, not really a system that could seriously make inroads into the FIH International competitions market. Yet, they sold like hotcakes !! In Britain, dozens were constructed by 1986, where a simplified "dynamic base"(not engineered, just layers of graded stone acted as the sub-structure) was commonplace with a geo-textile layer separating the stone from the carpet.

The carpet was piled high with sand, with the fibre tightly packed and in the initial stages, it did resemble a beach. Hockey-wise, the pace was often taken off the ball by a multitude of sand, the individual skills open to variation depending on the underlying density of sand, and indeed,the climatic condition of the day, whether wet or dry. After a while, these surfaces were susceptible to two more drawbacks, that of compaction and contamination.

Contamination from algae related growth took time, but compaction was felt early by this generation of both hockey and football players as a result of the scarcity of shock-pad materials below the carpet. Local Authorities in Britain were often sold on the premise of a multi sport, all weather pitch. Maybe, but without the quality, and sometimes because of the specification, without the physical support that this system ideally required. Ball bounce properties became a big issue as football clubs like Preston North End and Queens Park Rangers experienced comical trampolining of the football to uncontrollable heights.

Hockey also struggled at this stage between the two ends of the pendulum, appropriate ball bounce and player support and comfort. The technical problem in these early stages of the sand game, was that there desperately needed to be agencies, devoid of commercial affinity, that could be established to set up norms of ball speed, ball bounce and deviation. In addition, to also insist on a broad footing, the necessity to promote shock systems to prevent international generations from being old aged walking wounded clubs!! There was no doubt that the pioneer turf companies in sand really did try to promote the appropriate specifications, but, at this stage, equally, the under-surface mix was subject to some experimentation.

More turf companies sprung up with the Dutch and the British taking the lead. How did the Company sat away from this all, view the new scrambling to sand of its European competitors? Would they lower their prices? Would they indeed join the competition to get market share?

Ed Milner had some dilemmas to ponder over as Marketing Director of AstroTurf, would he let his nylon, shock pad product be pushed around by a polypropylene sanded Revolution Number 2 ? Ed was quite clear on this one, notably in his references on shock absorbency.

"We were aware of sand in-fills as early as 1979, as developed by Fred Haas, an old golf pro from New Orleans. His first efforts looked at golf greens. The early sand-filled systems were VERY hard. You had a sort of dry concrete with the sand particles embedded in a matrix of fibre. We visited them, observed and tested several institutions, but only in relation to American football. The hardness was just unacceptable.

Early visits to these sand facilities showed that the sand abraded the fibres with the abraded fibre particles washed out in rain storms leaving the seam quality at a very poor level. This advent of sand technology was overblown also when it came to shock absorbency which never matched the standards we were reaching with our engineered nylon systems. The measurement of cushioning properties was influenced by the Otto Graf Institute "Synthetic Athlete", as developed by Kolitzus resulting from work on running tracks for the 1936 Berlin Olympics.

At this stage, there was little reference to cushioning the head and neck of a real live sportsman in sport related impacts. Remember, here, in North

40

America, we felt it imperative to make system cushioning properties suitable for American football".

That sentiment,whether stated in these early pitch building days or espoused in modern day marketing must always be clearly understood as stated priorities for AstroTurf. They were American, and represented the corporate life of exchanging products in bulk for high capital reward. Monsanto were there to support field hockey's growth, but they also knew where their bread was buttered in the fifty one states of America, and that was firmly driven by grid iron football.

As Marketing Manager, Ed was well aware of the increasing interests of the world hockey market towards sand-filled installations. He was also impressed by Germany's interest in the sub strata to include shock pads equal to the same depth as the covering carpet. Negotiations took place and by the mid-eighties, Balsam A.G was responsible in Europe not only for marketing their Baspograss sand system fields, but also offering in addition the Rolls-Royce of pitches at their disposal, AstroTurf nylon.

It was a marketing stroke of genius. How did I know? Simply put, I was out there on the front line myself acting as a turf salesman with three varied samples to share with clients, the results of American and German technology combined. The Second Revolution was to be won by AstroTurf (with German assistance) on the combined Baspograss and nylon sales in the 80's decade with the Dutch combines working harder and harder to produce a middle of the range product in terms of performance, durability and cost. It was to take nearly another decade and into the twenty first century before quality polyethylenes would be broadly produced for the hockey market.

The proof that sand systems were not satisfying the hockey clientele was within the infill and in the quality of the polypropylene fibre as much as in the playing performance itself. The high infill that protected the fibre at birth was quickly eroded as rain,wind,abrasive footwear with a lack of coherent after care in the form of regular brushing meant that the surfaces were downgraded within five years. The heavy traffic of footballers in all types of footwear and in some environments the movement of the underlying strata from summer expansion and winter contraction also contributed to an inconsistent surface.

Technicians in Europe soon were answering the call for an upgrade in sand pitch installation with stringent targets in hockey for ball speed,deviation and bounce as well as a fundamental appraisal of the role of the shock pad in providing comfort where there had been little before. Pressure was not only being exerted by the hockey community,but also by the test laboratory centres of MSc in London, Sports Labs in Edinburgh and Labosport in Le Mans, France. These test houses were finding alarming disparities in the host of contractors and suppliers that were offering polypropylene products in terms of the hockey ball's interaction with the surface and its shock absorbency.

As so often happens, the upgrade was to take a significant nudge from another sport, which was, of course ,football. The French training centre for football under the watchful eye of Gerard Houllier had been experimenting with the french carpet supplier, Tarket, which had supplied higher standard polyethylene fibre, one third of the sand infill with a 12-15 m.m pad to control the ball bounce whilst affording a real cushion for football. By 1998, both lab and field tests by Sports Labs had supported the theory that it was easily possible to have a surface suitable for soccer and hockey.

This truly was the extra time winner for the European manufacturers as they all now climbed into the polyethylene market with a vengeance offering assertive marketing methods, some interesting claims of hybrid, wet and dry systems, even offering multi-colour run-offs and pitches to the dedicated followers of fashion. Did they play better - yes ;were they less abrasive,no, as top fibre dry still left marks!! Did they last longer-- no, but you had more years of quality. Were they less expensive -- no !!

The second half of the sand revolution brought us less sand and more marketable products, but it would be a misnomer to call it a revolution, more of an evolution from an inauspicious beginning back in the mid eighties. It has ,however, lasted through to the current day with the majority of sales in Europe for hockey for companies like TigerTurf, Greenfields, Edel Grass and Desso being directed into the polyethylene sector.

For Ed Milner, he now had led AstroTurf through these dynamic changes in surface technology and,indeed, in the game of hockey itself. He retired in 1991 still very active in consultative work, but also to the end, firm in the belief that sand was never the answer to further the sport of hockey. Many readers out there who played and lived through the "Second Generation of Hockey surfaces" would definitely agree that they were never ideal, but they were very much affordable, and answered the need of European clubs and schools to own their own facility.

Those same readers would hold Mr. Milner and his American cohorts responsible for the high cost of their products, which forced hockey Club Chairmen into the welcoming grasping hands of the sand moguls!!

So, where did the hockey purists stand on these issues? How did Sand change the nature and standard of play every weekend around the world? The FIH never supported its use at International tournament level, insisting on the exclusive use of water, despite huge environmental complaints from the lobbyists. The 1990's saw AstroTurf take on the Lahore and Sydney World Cups and the Barcelona and Atlanta Olympics with only the Dutch supplying a Desso home product for the '98 Utrecht World Cup. There emerged by the millennium an enormous gap between the haves and the have -nots in every respect, but primarily caused by the divisive nature of the two "Astro revolutions". In external competitions, those nations that had invested heavily in the original water-filled nylon product, notably Germany, Australia, Spain, Pakistan and Great Britain achieving tremendous successes between 1988 and 2000 at the majors of Olympics and Junior and Senior World Cups.

However, the poorer nations of Asia, Africa and South America were blown off the hockey map, including former giants India and Kenya, as well as former solid Euro-nations, Poland, Russia and Belgium. Soon, there emerged a super hierarchy of three privileged countries who would literally confiscate the spoils of victory to The Hague World Cup and beyond. The rich just got richer on the back of the technology of turf.

Yet, it was not only in external competition that sporting elites were developing, they were within countries themselves. Inside FIH nations from New Zealand through Asia to even the hockeycrats of Europe, the stark fact was exposed for all to see, that if you did not bring your club members up on water turfs, and in particular your youth development, you were dead in the sand!! It was no use offering a bog standard sand-filled polypropylene to aspiring players anymore. They would just give you a wry smile and walk away to the nearest "oasis in the desert". They were seeking water, with the skills of water which demanded vertical and horizontal techniques of trapping, tackling and passing.

Sand had for a generation almost necessitated the technical use of low horizontal skills, the use of the common flat stick tackle, and had exhibited the slower pace associated with many sand-filled games. It was almost as if the game had come full circle with the range of skills equating to what we had all left behind all those years ago on grass. Sand had merely been a rather circuitous bridge between grass to water turf in the use of a wide variety of game skills. Of course there would be in the modern era of the last few years a move to rubber technology, the third generation, but this would just not take off for hockey.

Nevertheless, what it has done is replace all those older sand-filled surfaces to meet the demands of multi sport in Local Authority areas (football small team game zones) leaving even less hockey specific pitches in the crowded urban centres of Europe. Countries like France, Spain, Ireland and notably Britain, you today in 2015, will see fewer and fewer hockey facilities in city centres. The sport has moved to the well-off outer suburbs ensuring that hockey today in the USA and Europe has become an upper-middle class sport, expensive bordering on elitism. Back in city centres with the problems of security,pollution and vandalism, no AstroTurf 5 or System 90 would survive. Yes, a sorry condemnation on the modern developed urban core and its football dominated inhabitants.

Yet, I wonder whether Ed Milner would ever have thought it would come to this!! To be sure, that he not only as the premier leader of the Turf Revolution in laboratory technology would transform the sport of hockey, but also redefine the location of where we played the game in the world of our inner cities today!!

Ed Milner, the AstroTurf Guru, receives his commendation medal from FIH President, Etienne Glititch

Playing on redgra shale in Barcelona in 1972

The modern water-filled scene

Canadian
Field
Hockey
Association

Eight Nations
Tournament

L'Association
Canadienne
de Hockey
sur Gazon

Le tournoi
des huit nations

Mr. W.H. Israel,
Mr E.M.Milner,
Monsanto Co.,
800 N. Lindbergn Blvd.,
St Loius,
Missouri,

7 Madawaska Dr.,
Ottawa,
K1S 3G5
Ont.

August 26th, 1975

Gentlemen,

Attached is the second of statistics on the Montreal 8 Nations Tournament. The first lot of raw data you received when we met. I have rewritten the article "Penalty Corners Win Matches? ", which will be published in our national magazine shortly. You now have the comparison between 2 tournaments on grass and one on Astroturf. As you will see by my final comment my enthusiasm for the surface is apparent. It is nonsheless disturbing to see the effect that the nap of the turf (north to south) is having on a key element of the game, namely the penalty corner. It forced teams to take their penalty corners from the side with the nap, in preference to the natural position to the right of the goalkeeper. I was concerned when all the corners were added up that perhaps there was an aberration in the data, but by averages, there should be the same number of penalty corners at each end (split evenly for the 151 studied) – but the number of goals was different.

As to your question on the time contribution of ball boy/girls this is hard to estimate. Based on a sample of 4 matches involving each team (8), the average time for 514 free hits was 7.1 sec, whereas the push ins was 5.5 secs on 205 times. Except for free hits over the goal line, or over the side line (few), the ball girls are not usually involved, in getting play restarted. If a weighted average of 0.4 secs for free hits is the required contribution by ball girls, then the difference is 2.0 secs between an adjusted free hits with NO ballgirls and free push ins with ball girls. Provided there is a good outer net screen system, there is no inherent reason why push ins should take less time than free hits. With these broad assumptions and estimates, I calculate the contribution of ballgirls to have been 44 secs/match for free hits, and 91 secs for push ins (seems a bit low by gut feel). With the average playing time of 43

75

International
Competitions
Montreal 1975

Competitions
internationales
Montréal 1975

Secrétariat
155 est, rue Notre-Dame
Montréal, Que., Canada
h3C 3A6

This page and next: The first Olympics on turf - the Canadian Secretary expresses doubts!!

minutes in 1975 per match, and an often quoted figure of 32 minutes on grass (seems high - I prefer 26 mins), then the contribution of artificial turf could be calculated to be 7 minutes per match. This is indeed a very sizable contribution as a percentage - 22%. This is certainly an important ingredient to the promotion of the game as a spectator sport.

In the attached documents you will find a Highlights section. Again the total whistles are well down.

Watering has to be a major area for further investigation as it affects the ball and the run of it. How resilient is the turf to having a watering truck pass over the field and spray the field - this would be more even than the hosing technique used in 1975. As your photos showed the patchwork effect is definitely undesirable. Suitable rates of application would be required in the time available at half time (5-8 minutes.)

I have included some photocopies of work sheets that may be of interest to you. I shall be looking further at the data for a number of other areas in September/October. Maybe we can discuss further at the Pan American Games in Mexico City. I trust that we have now fullfilled our part in supply of the basic details of artificial turf. I shall be in Calgary this weekend for the nationals and will try to record a couple of games for comparison sake, on grass.

After a hectic August completing my extensive report to COJO, and a house move as well, it has been a hard job to get all the various hockey outlets dealt with.

I look forward to hearing of any further analysis that you may do, or wish to be done.

Yours very truly,

Denys G.T.Cooper.

INTERNATIONAL HOCKEY FEDERATION Internationale de Hockey

RENE G. FRANK

6th April, 1982

Monsanto Europe
Avenue de Tervuren 270/272 (Box 1)
1150 BRUSSELS

Attention Mr F. Schelkens
Manager Europe - Africa
Recreational Products

Dear Mr Schelkens,

In accordance with your wish, I take pleasure in confirming that ASTROTURF Synthetic Grass produced by MONSANTO, is suitable for hockey competitions at the highest level, including the Olympic Games, the World Cup, the Champions Trophy and the Intercontinental Cup.

With kind regards,

Yours sincerely,

Rene G. Frank
President

This is a true and correct copy of the original document in our Brussels files.

E. M. Milner

Notary Public

Signed and sealed this 22nd day of April, 1982.

1 - Avenue des Arts, 1040 BRUXELLES (Belgique) ☎ (2) 218.45.37 - ✦ Inthockey Bruxelles - Telex 63393 FIH b

Full approval for AstroTurf in 1982 from the FIH

-Part D-
The Future is Video

The modern International Tournament is an open affair. Everywhere in the stadia, you will see cameras and personal devices to record the moment. High in the viewing arena, normally behind the goals, the hockey enthusiasts will be impressed by a multitude of digitised National Team equipment filming the matches. Their combined budgets to gain the technical advantage run into millions.

Yet, given the current state of notational analysis, how many of these hockey technocrats will have heard of Steven Faaronheigt. More than any of them, or any national grouping, he contributed in formulating the base and the growth of video methodology and camera technique for the sport of hockey.

Unusual name, that is clear, but another example of an estranged family that left their Austrian home at the torrid time of the Second World War to set up in California. Like many migrants, the family had subtly changed their name which had previously sounded like a meteorological condition. Steven was a second generation migrant who had weathered the storms of Vietnam Conflict and the West Coast hippie culture, and come out the other side to discover a true affinity with film, cameras, analysis, and the lifestyle associated with Southern California.

At first he found pick up work in small edit suites which provided background footage for small scale documentaries within the burgeoning television industry of Los Angeles. Hollywood had supported numerous derivative small film companies around the region which had worked hand in glove with the major networks.

By the early 1980s, a settled community had set the scene over five decades for the biggest film concentration in the world, and this was not lost on the Los Angeles 1984 Olympic Organising Committee, nor on the rather eccentric, but brilliant video technician called Steven Faaronheigt. Originally, Betamax and the Betacam SP system was able to act as master tape to the then-recently marketed and modernised VHS video tape.

This offshoot of mass production was to dominate the ever-demanding individual and commercial use of programming for the following decade and a half. Therefore, technology had met human expertise at a focal point at the same time. The time was 1984, the place was Los Angeles, the people were already steeped in film, and the event was the Olympic Games.

Hockey, of course, had been filmed in the past but not broadly used for match analysis and preparation, rather more for entertainment purposes. Cine-film never really was able to provide adequate close-ups or wide-field views from single positions, and the coaches up until the 1980s were rather reluctant to delve into technology as a potential aid to their knowledge and normal routines with the players. Equally, hockey cameramen were few and far between, so therefore, it was often a soccer or American football cameraman that until then were spotted behind the camera lens.

Steven, or Stevo as he was known, had over a period of eighteen years acquired the discipline of filming, writing scripts, and cutting and splicing material to form extended film programmes. His was a classic story of do it yourself and learn from experiences both good and bad. He knew the Olympics was about to hit town within 12 months and as a keen American football fan, he also recognised that all Olympic coaches would be more than open to receive the potential benefits of competing in "Tinseltown." Indeed he had proffered advice for the first time to build up in the Olympic villages a Video Library which coaches and managers could use to view specific events at the prospective Games on a daily basis.

A control desk would be set up in a specific building to be connected to a huge network of TV screens which would play back the race, bout, or match that had been contested that very day. For Olympic coaches, it was a first, as was the use of headphones during matches which linked the head coach at pitch-side with his coaching staff high in the stands. The Los Angeles Organising Committee, superbly lead by Peter Uberoth, was to liaise very cleverly and with great attention to detail with operatives like Stevo who knew the film business inside out. The Library was a static concept, but brilliant in reality because material was tightly monitored from a central control tower. Flexibility was afforded the coaches in their cubicles, where the VHS recorder provided them with freeze frame facilities through the 'pause' mechanism on the recorder. The material, owned by the TV network, was totally secure and protected as the tape was returned to the Librarian after use as a precondition of hire.

Stevo had more ideas. He wanted to work directly with an American Olympic team and get involved with the Olympic process and experience. He was not going to let an Olympiad come to his home town without his positive involvement! The film guru had been technically part of the support staff to a very popular programme on TV at the time called "Bleeps and Bloopers", essentially a fun-time score on disasters, errors, and slap-stick mistakes which were essentially comical in nature.

He researched such a project involving only Olympic sports and suggested to Executives that the network could source such material by seeking any available footage from the head coaches of the dozens of sports that made up the American Olympic teams. Executives could invite the top Men's and Women's coaches down to either of their Hollywood or Burbank studios to discuss the concept and use of "the Olympic Bleeps and Bloopers" programme, and indeed for them to meet the technicians to draw up the detail in a positive televised light.

The response was tremendous from the coaches, but there was one guy who Stevo felt he could work with beyond the concept of "Bleeps and Bloopers", and move into the filming, editing, and production of film in his particular sport. He was the head coach of the USA Men's Field Hockey Squad, Gavin Featherstone.

Featherstone had brought along four specific cuts of hockey film which he had acquired over the years, which had amounted to embarrassing open goals spurned, to explicit views of players' underwear after falling, and to punch-up altercations!

"I offered the material and these guys responded with the language of Hollywood, words like 'awesome', 'sensational' and 'stellar'. It was a different world! But there was one technician who stuck out as more than a boffin, he was a real pro. He gave me his card, and as they say, the rest is history," said Featherstone.

Indeed it was not long before Stevo had ingratiated himself into the United States Men's programme for the Olympic Games. There was neither budget nor open association for him, but on a part-time basis, he was happy to have that Olympic label attached to the work assigned to him over the next two years. It was clear that Featherstone was cautious about the role that Stevo was about to play. He needed to know that the Californian could film training, and cut and splice that material with International footage to produce a final master tape of visual and sound quality. The Head Coach, up in Ventura County, regularly held open video evenings at a local Italian restaurant for his Olympic squad and stable of junior coaches.

The filming was easy for Stevo as he had been behind the lens before in various sports, but he knew he had to take specific advice from the hockey man on angles, sudden changes of the ball's direction, and the trickier track on aerial play and passes. These camera skills were readily acquired at the weekend training sessions for the squad at East Los Angeles College, the venue for the Olympic hockey event. Equally, Featherstone wanted to assess his edit suite facilities and Stevo's capacity to produce reliable video reproductions. The only way to reassure the coach was to invite him down to "The Shack"—as he called it—in Malibu, the film capital's coastal playground. "The Shack" was Stevo's apartment. It was a three-room apartment, one room an edit studio, the second an audio dub box which doubled as a bathroom, and a bedroom which overlooked the Pacific Ocean.

"After that day it was clear to both of us that we could form a partnership, a company that could make hockey films for a long time to come," said the Head Coach in April 1984.

Faaronheigt regarded the sport as being dull. Its coverage needed sprucing up with multiple angles, slow motions capturing slide actions on the water filled surface, close-up shots of goalkeepers, and amplifying the sounds of the game at pitch-side level. There followed close interaction between the network covering the Games, with Stevo, and Featherstone in how Olympic hockey should be filmed. Most of Stevo's suggestions were taken on board apart from his fixation with accompanying hockey action with music from the West Coast sounds of which he was a devoted admirer! The Games was a startling success with many notables stating that hockey had broken new ground in its coverage of the Olympics in Los Angeles.

The film guru did not stop there! Featherstone had become increasingly interested in the workings of the edit suite and in the end product to release coaching films on a whole range of hockey topics. The two of them had discussed at some length that as long as they had access to quality International hockey footage (that was relatively easy at that time), they could press ahead with creative use of advanced technology to expand coaching ideas and training.

Note, at this time in 1984, there had not been any commercial videos on the market as a concerted effort to present hockey coaching in any form to young players or adults alike. The two of them had at their disposal the assets of slow-motion, freeze frame labelling, superimposing lines, arrows, and split-screens of all shapes and sizes. Faaronheigt had the tools of his trade, Featherstone had the hockey knowledge, experience, and vision of where to go.

There was just one big problem. Stevo was a true son of California who had lived life to the full for nearly two decades. He was an early surfer, but physical exercise had been replaced by sensory stimulation of almost anything that was nearly illegal. His substance abuse and full-time womanising was, with every year, eating into him as compulsive daily habits. It was becoming serious.

The American Head Coach always kept Stevo away from his Olympic squads and the expanding Southern Californian Youth Programme, and the reasons were obviously now quite clear to see. Featherstone was not to renew his contract with the American Men's group after the Olympics in 1985, but he did invite Stevo to the UK to form a new video company specialising in the making of a series termed "Hockey in the 80s".

Tragically that amazing double act was never to materialise. Stevo's health nose-dived into rapid decline, and after refusing to leave his California home for a new challenge in London, six months later he passed away. Hockey never knew this Californian so far removed from the sport's focal points around the world, but he had lit the fuse for one hockey professional who was to create the longest running video and DVD series for hockey over two decades.

That was Steven Faaronheigt's real legacy. Gavin Featherstone carried the torch for Stevo, the man he described as having more creative talent in his fingertips than any player he had ever coached. "Hockey in the 80s" produced four tapes: "Hockey for Juniors," "Hockey for Goalkeepers," "Hockey the Modern Game," and "Hockey for Umpires," which were exported to all five continents with startling sales.

He was now followed by a great deal of movement as National Associations aligned with influential sponsors were preparing to place their own VHS-format tapes in front of an increasingly hungry hockey world. The two notable tapes that were marketed in English onto a world market were England Hockey's "Play Hockey Slazenger Style", and Australia's Esanda sponsored product "The Skills Revolution."

Rather more general in content as both these tapes covered the broad spectrum of differing skills, the videos portrayed top International players performing the base skills as they were prioritised in England and Australia. This was a very important new step for video in hockey as it really displayed the power of video transmission to all corners of these two nations. For a mere $30, or £20, a tiny school or club anywhere could buy into the training and coaching of its National philosophy which was deemed essential for all players to progress. All from a seat on the sofa at home.

In schools now, the teachers of the game, so severely starved of material in the past, had some core principles to work from as well as a wet-weather program!

It undoubtedly helped to see the stars of the game as role models in training. David Whitaker, the British Olympic Coach and Richard Aggiss, his Los Angeles Games Australian rival, were quick to utilise the demonstration skills of the stars of the day, Sean Kerly, Ian Taylor, Paul Barber, and in Perth, of Rick Charlesworth, Jim Irvine, and Terry Walsh.

Thus, within two years of the LA Games, video had hit the world's classrooms and those pupils both in Australia and England would have noticed that the ensuing World Cup Final of 1986 in London was between the same two nations. They also will have observed that all the demonstrations on these early coaching tapes were carried out on either sand or water-filled synthetic turf.

Video, notably in the facilities shown and in the types of skills development executed on these tapes, was acting to expand the game and its future expectations for the sport to be played at all levels on these new surfaces. Whereas "Slazenger Style" and "Skills Revolution" were one-off VHS tapes, Gavin Featherstone's tapes were out-selling both as he delved into specialised areas of the sport with each succeeding title.

The Englishman sought out and understood the ongoing connection between synthetic turf and video. The proof of the pudding was his teaming up with Balsam A.G., a German synthetic supplier of mainly sand-filled systems.

From the commercial point of view, how effective was it in the late 80s for a turf company to be in partnership with an International coach that plied his trade through video?

Kevin Rylett was central to the Balsam operations in England as heading up the technical side of installing mainly sand filled systems. His account reflects the busiest time in building British hockey synthetic fields:

"Ironically it all originated from the Winterbottom Report at the start of the decade in association with RAPRA(the Rubber and Plastics Research Association) wherein football at top club level was looking into the use of synthetic surfaces. In the industry, there was already considerable debate at what should underlie these new polypropylene carpets, in short whether they should have a dynamic, or have an engineered layer beneath the carpet.

We were thinking about the support system for the athlete's body, but when certain systems exposed a crazy ball bounce as at Queens Park Rangers and Preston, the synthetic pitch industry took a bad rap from all the football authorities. From the start with football, we were off on the wrong foot. Still, the pitch-building industry expanded through the 80's as there developed a great deal of interest from hockey. It was timely when Gavin Featherstone contacted us in 1986 to arrange a meeting.

The meeting was simply dynamite for us. Gavin demonstrated through his Hockey Video Series the ability to simultaneously advertise our latest pitch products. He showed through close up slow motions the interaction of ball and surface, the pace and bounce of the ball. Believe me, it reflected very well on our product and with our background pitch banners and the detailed dedication at the end of the tape, Balsam was besieged with enquiries for years in the future. We had never seen video for hockey before then, but the way he presented it to us and his subsequent shows around the country was ahead of anyone in the sport, even his own National Association.

Even the titles 'Hockey: The Modern Game', 'Hockey for Coaches' and 'Hockey for Juniors' were directed at the very market our sales personnel were most actively attacking. The period from 1986 to 1990 was definitely our busiest with installations, and with the Great Britain men's team winning an Olympic Gold, these were days where hockey had been pushed to the forefront of all schools, colleges and clubs throughout the land. We continued to sponsor Gavin for another five years both here in England and in his Overseas tours. He definitely made the name of Balsam synonymous with the game's expansion and our profit margins!!"

Video was, remember, a new technology in schools, but like many innovations it was to take time to take hold. How was it to be incorporated into a school or club's sports schedule and in some cases, schools did not have the budget to invest into it as quickly as they would have liked. The private sector did move more hastily, and with more time available in the evenings at boarding schools, were able to host coaching clinics around the television in the winter nights.

It was still unusual at this time to notice any practical widespread use of video at club or school level anywhere in the hockey world. However, in International hockey, video operatives were starting to appear with increasingly more elaborate equipment that took up far too much room in some shared video platforms at major events! Some nations, notably Holland and Germany, were well ahead of the game by employing part-

time video specialists specifically attached to their National teams at all
levels for men and women.

In other cases such as England and Australia, they either trained up their
goalkeeper or assistant coaches to conduct the all-important camera work
in the day times and the arduous editing work at night. The editing, in the
pre-digital world, was a painstaking part of the job depending on what the
Head Coach required, and it was not unusual for assistant coaches to be
putting in night shifts of four hours or more to have material ready for the
Head Coach's perusal at breakfast. Indeed, the finished product often could
have been only ten to fifteen minutes of selected, highlighted footage.
The hockey use of video continued in this vein much through the 90s with
the coach's attention often shifting on to individual and team analysis
of opposing teams. It would stay the same as long as there were no
specific strides in visual technology which would alter the way we would
approach the game. Certainly more and more Associations were now
completing plans to utilise promotional or coaching theory videos in the
commercial sector both to spread ideas of their coaching methodology to
their membership and as a source of revenue streams into the coaching
budgets.

Featherstone meanwhile was ploughing on with his new "Hockey in the
90s" series contributing seven more tapes for the International market.
Essentially he had established major agents world-wide, for the Americas,
South Africa, and Australasia, whilst he himself conducted open clinics
and business events and tours in Europe and Asia. These "road shows"
were novel and had attracted large audiences of coaches and teachers
who could openly debate the content of the videos with the Director of
the Series himself. As in the business world generally, visual impact had
become a potent force as presentation then required interesting video
material to attract a client or customer to any innovative new product.

The former American coach had pioneered these formats of presentation
in hockey which were, after his initial shows from as early as 1986, to be
quite commonplace amongst National Associations later to follow his
lead in gaining greater direct access to their teachers of the game. As we
have seen, the world of hockey video was not just helping the players and
coaches, but had a direct impact on surfacing, facilities, communications,
and it acted as a major force in globalisation in making ideas accessible
across borders, indeed making the hockey world a much smaller place.

By the end of the century, the video phenomenon needed a boost. The
VHS format was getting stale and everything in technology was becoming
smaller, more portable, and more compact for the individual to handle.

Like Betamax and Betacam before it, soon the VHS tape had outlived its shelf life, the world was to go digital!

At this juncture it was vital to understand what role Head Coaches had in mind for video technology at the top end of the game. It was noticeable by 2000 and the Sydney Olympics that the developed world had taken advantage of the various elements of the hockey dynamic to lead the world of hockey. Rid of earlier restrictions which were suspicious of interaction between the sporting, technical, and commercial corners of the game, the National Governing Bodies were far more inclined to absorb sponsorship and business attachments to bolster the accompanying technology to assist the coaches in the sport.

Many National teams were, as the term explained, Coach led. The implications of this development were to file straight into the video world for not just in analysis but also in the entertainment side of hockey as well. Certainly in Holland, Argentina, and parts of Australia like Tasmania and Western Australia, there were regular weekly hockey programmes which were now available to an eager public. Programmes meant editors, cameramen, edit technicians, and audio dubbing and commentators. Hockey was building up its own areas of expertise connected to video and outside broadcasting.

In England, Sky TV had run an earlier Pilot TV show with Nick Irvine as the genial anchor man in commentating on the "match of the day" centralised at Birmingham University between two National League Men's club teams. Sky invited a seasoned hockey personality to accompany the enthusiastic Irvine for the Sunday matches.

The experiment lasted for just one season as the £1000 paid to, yes to, Sky Sports per show was put forward by one of hockey's grandees, Peter Boizot of Pizza Express fame. The games were centralised with spectators bussed in to support their own teams in the highest league in England.

Irvine presented with verve, and with an expertise not experienced before, and with coaching experts aside him, he definitely produced a positive background to the play. The pilot scheme bombed as Pizza Express's new management were less than impressed as a result of poor live audience attendances. Hockey, in England, despite a professional product, was not supported by its member participants nor, more pointedly, by its governing body, then The Hockey Association, who just tamely backed away from television.

Both in Holland and Argentina the responses were very different. Without having to compete for a National audience that were fanatical in their support for the expanding English Premier Football League and a highly popular "Rugby Special" programme, hockey filled the void in a much needed way in these two successful hockey nations. In both cases, success was evident with the continuing medal count of the Dutch at World Cups and Olympics, and Argentina offered particularly with Las Leonas, the Women's squad, a modern hockey culture that was competing for gold with the Oranje from The Netherlands. Their programmes were well researched with a full coverage of the top club hockey from Buenos Aires and Amsterdam, but what was obvious from the start was the investment that terrestrial television had placed in the product. There was a total professionalism in the camera work both outside and inside the studio, a triumph for the role of video in hockey and the guarded financial support it was receiving.

Of course, this all married up very well with the broad use of digitised material. Coaches were enthusiastic about the exposure that hockey was starting to gain, but where the digital revolution really made an impact was in match analysis. With the increasing number of young coaches coming from a sports science background in their University studies, match statistics and figures were playing an increasing part in the coach's assessment of how his or her players were performing.

Rightly or wrongly, coaches were interested—some totally obsessed-- by analysis sheets which would supply, for example, the spatial runs of the strikers, the peripheral ball distribution of centre midfields, or the number of circle-penetrations of each respective striker. They were not just curious about spatial patterns, but most significantly, about the time these patterns had occurred during a game. Was there, for instance, a concentration of activity in the first or the last quarter of the game? The coaches could now quantify the trends of play for their own team and opponent alike.

For sure, we were entering the modern age and the desire for information and detail to be disseminated at source, an immediate flow of data and comparative data from previous games was soon to be made available to the coach. Indeed this final stage of video analysis would be taken out of the heads of the hockey coach. He or she now could buy into multinational systems that could be applied across a whole variety of sports. It became a question of how the big concerns like Game Breaker and Dartfish could apply their latest computer technology to a whole range of parallel sports. The machines were taking over!

Hockey coaches were to change in the decade leading to the 2014 World Cup for men and women in The Hague. Their eyes, ears, and brains had been superseded by the multitude of instant options that a computer programme could now incorporate. The coach and his staff had to be computer literate and intrinsically believe that statistics, flowcharts, and data introspection were to be the way forward to improved performance for the modern athlete and team player.

All computers achieved one common asset: they saved time. The digital revolution at the turn of the century would now offer hockey coaches this huge advantage. There was to be immediate video feedback, instant replays without breaking ongoing action. The coach could, by viewing on two separate windows, actually code material whilst capturing footage. In dealing with individual players, it was straight forward to analyse trends from differing matches and by gathering up the excerpts attach coaching notes to the clips: indeed, compile short, personalised player tapes.

Two of the leading companies to supply these options for hockey coaches have been Game Breaker and Dartfish, both of whom have inbuilt programmes which can monitor player movements and distances covered in a game to provide a no-hiding-place for the player! The detail of such can be downloaded and sent to the player on a DVD, email, or iPod.

Hence the digitised revolution really with its tagging, zoom boxes, and Track performance features represented the advanced stage of the role of video in terms of analysis and the formulation of video programmes. With a world finely tuned to computer generated technology, hockey and other team sports had moved onto a new plane.

Everything became more standardised with National Coaching bodies able to produce coaching tapes at will with a high-end budget in coaching development. Nations like The Netherlands were able to gain backing from world economic powers like Royal Dutch Shell to sponsor their outgoing hockey materials to an ever-faithful home market of teachers and coaches.

Individual enterprise was still present as Gavin Featherstone pushed ahead with a new International series on styles of play entitled "The Team Coaching Series". It contained five separate tapes assessing the virtues of Australian, Argentinian, Dutch, Asian, and Chinese play with some very interesting innovations within an interactive framework. The series was fully endorsed by the FIH Coaching Committee which, under the heading of Advanced Technical and Tactical Material, was especially pleased that the coaching content spread across the globe with International co-

commentators providing a real variety of views and perspectives on the game. It also introduced "Hock-Eye" from which a live single camera shot from a centre line position could snap shot a skill or movement, then by "moving the camera", assess the captured movement from a totally different pitch angle.

The series was acquired much more by National Associations than by individual hockey enthusiasts as in the hay days of VHS. Yet, here was the rub. Digitised developments were technically superb but less personalised as models and data began to replace the human element of the game. Featherstone himself knew that this was the twenty-year end and farewell to his involvement with presenting video programmes for clients all over the world. Now with an Apple Computer and with a little bit of patience, any techno could produce a hockey programme of sorts in a day with their own iMovie facility.

Rather like the creative musicians in the pop industry, recording was neither fulfilling nor profitable as so much material was downloaded instantly by clients at original source material quality. The musicians went back to playing live shows, Featherstone returned to active team coaching, on the field!!

The machines were ready to take over, but one had to be concerned with the invisible people behind the computers. Were they really hockey coaches or computer programmers applying rudimentary rules of statistics to team sports? It was David Whitaker who rightly said in his excellent book "The Hockey Workshop," that one of the major resources any coach has is his own mind. It is there to provide solutions and options in order to offer a firm foundation of principles for players to consider.

This author firmly believes that too much analysis spells paralysis, and that Head Coaches should be very selective in how they use video in the future. They have an instant and overwhelming amount of physical evidence today to try to cut through to provide the players with clear objectives. The coaches must note that human communication both on and off the field of play is worth a goal to any team at any level. A reliance of the players on personalised iPods and individual programmes does not enhance team understanding and does not prioritise on the field the vital decision making processes that all players must make at vital times in match play.

Deeper than this, our old mate Steven Faaronheigt had dared to suggest that the game was dull, and he wanted to see more entertainment, more music, more chance, and more action. He definitely led this approach from the front. Never did he, nor any of us, want to see a third Umpire stuck in the stands adjudicating whether the ball struck a foot in the circle whilst the players stood around for a minute awaiting their fate. That represented modern day nonsense in the use of video, when such good rule changes like self-start had given the game more fun and flow.

The game of hockey desperately needs to look in on itself as it is becoming a slave to technology in the training, coaching, and playing elements of the sport. Video had provided a firm base as a support, I stress, support system to the main facets of the game. No one wants, at any level, the game being denigrated to a chess encounter, and hockey is at many levels today subject to that trend line.

We take too much for granted in this great sport, and hockey enthusiasts the world over can often state the obvious with sweeping generalisations. Many times has it been broadcast that hockey as a sport has never gripped the three most powerful nations on the globe: Russia, China, and America. The latter has, in general, been inward looking with its hockey and has not made a major human impact in terms of International prowess at any level. True, a deficit in the areas of competitive hockey on the playing, coaching, and achievement side, but just look how the United States has shaped and moulded Field Hockey from the technical and technological standpoints.

These last two chapters have demonstrated that the surfaces that have evolved from the original AstroTurf advanced polymer technology and the revised video systems that have covered the sport as a spectacle have been two vital cogs in "The Hockey Dynamic".

From the small beginnings in a tiny Georgia town and from "The Shack" in Malibu, Ed Milner and Steven Faaronheigt did more than their fair share to advance the cause of hockey with their technical wizardry. Now, it had to be the turn of David Whitaker's "brains trust", The Coaches, to take the game to the next level, and they were all just sitting there ready and waiting across the Atlantic Ocean!

GAVIN FEATHERSTONE

Olympic Coach to the U.S.A. team in Los Angeles, has trained teams in four continents over the last decade. Born in England, and educated at Durham and Oxford Universities, he had the distinction of captaining England at all three levels – Schools, Junior and Senior during the 1970's.

He was on Millfield's Staff as Head Coach between 1977-79 and continued to work with Universities, Clubs and Representative teams from as far afield as New Delhi, New York, Singapore and Amsterdam.

In 1982 he was given the challenging post of coaching the U.S.A. Men's Team for the Pan American and Olympic Games. His efforts took the National Teams to some startling results in 1984 with the U.S.A. gaining their first victories over European nations and creditable draws with Kenya and Malaysia.

Gavin received his coaching qualifications from the English H.A. and has acted as chief examiner for the Hockey Association Coaching Gradings. He recently was chief organiser for the F.I.H. (Pan American) Coaching Course in 1985 but now resides in England as a Consultant Coach, notably in Preparatory and Secondary Schools.

HOCKEY IN THE 80'S

HOCKEY for JUNIORS

CONTACT:
Gavin Featherstone

HOCKEY IN THE 80'S
HOCKEY for JUNIORS

The second series has been aimed at Junior levels of Hockey. It places emphasis on the period of early coaching in players first two or three years in the game. Mr. Featherstone attaches great importance to teaching skills in a mobile context and that skills should cover or isolated into compartments e.g. Dribbling and Hitting to Combined Skills.

Explanation of each topic has been designed with the most modern technical methods of video screening and presentation. The teacher/player is then introduced to practice demonstrations by both Men and Women Representative players and by 11-13 year old youngsters. All these locals are therefore exposed to the same techniques in practise. All topics are enhanced by 5 minute sequences from International Outdoor and Indoor Hockey – a Coaching commentary describes in detail the importance of each part supported by freeze-frame and action replay facility.

The five topics are:
1. GRIP – stick skill.
2. FOOTWORK – hit/push.
3. SCRIMMAGE – small team practise.
4. TACKLING – win the ball.
5. GOALSCORING – indoor influences.

1. GRIP – stick skill.

The video shows the relationship between the grip of the stick and the fast deceptive movement of the ball on the stick. Practicing players will display their abilities on their reverse sticks. It is stressed that fast side skills must be encouraged at an early age with as much mobility and agility applied to practising exercises. The excerpt from International Hockey covers the brilliant stick handling skills of Stephan Blöcher of West Germany in competition against Holland.

2. FOOTWORK – hit and push.

This section advocates the teaching of hit and push skills off both feet. Very few young players are instructed how to play the ball off their right foot. It is essential to make youngsters aware that they have to play the ball at the correct time and that they must distribute off the feet that is leading at that time. This opens up many more options for players and the study of Holland's Women's Olympic Gold Medalists demonstrates how much footwork plays in the success of their play.

3. SCRIMMAGE – small team practise.

It is essential for teachers to break down the 11-a-side game to limited area small team games. This practise gives each individual player more involvement in the game and each game is designed to encourage the development of each skills as passing, hitting, scooping and scoring goals. The International game covered features the precision passing and skills execution of Olympic Silver Medallists West Germany and Europa Cup Champions Holland.

4. TACKLING – win the ball.

This section deals with one of the most difficult skills for young players to master, that of TACKLING. The ability to feint, delay and channel are carefully considered with much stress placed upon footwork and body positioning. Players practise various approaches to TACKLING in mobile situations that require fast thinking and positive defending. Finally, Mr. Featherstone analyses the value and contribution of indoor techniques when applied to outdoor international play.

5. GOALSCORING – indoor influences.

This final section deals with the aspect of Hockey all young players enjoy – scoring goals. Mr. Featherstone shows some important techniques in scoring, analysing the value of limited backswing, extended pushes, lifted plays and rounding the keeper. He places great emphasis upon, and recognises the value of the Indoor game in perfecting these skills. The exercises bring out the best of the finishing talents of the practising players. These same techniques are shown up dramatically from the match-play sequences from the top Indoor competition in the World, in West Germany.

The first video training and coaching series, circa 1988

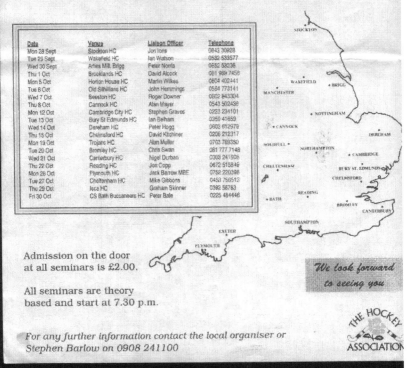
How England Hockey used the videos by Roadshows, 1992

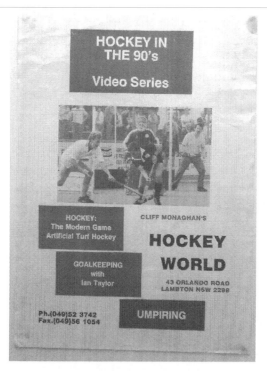

The videos are marketed Down Under

*World hockey styles are examined,
with FIH approval*

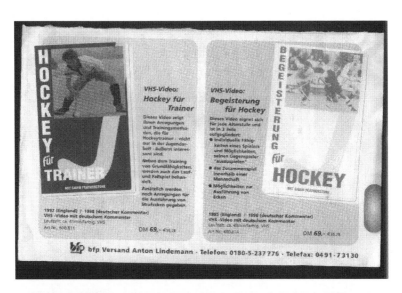

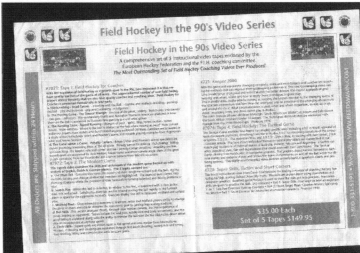

The series translated into German and American

-Part E-
Coaches Take the Lead

As hockey was to push forward through the advent of technology, it still needed a firm base on which to prosper. Coaching or the appliance of technical emphasis in coaching had been slowly introduced throughout the 1960's, but it really burst upon the scene as an organised entity in Europe from 1970.

Before exploring the solid foundation laid down on that decade, it is vital to trace the reasons why it had occurred at this time in particular. Throughout Europe but notably in Britain, Holland, Belgium and Spain, the club was the focal point for any playing or organisational development in hockey. If guidance was required in playing terms, the clubs seldom looked past team captains or at best on an off the field manager who really doubled as a 'Bags' man for kit and a hockey confidante to the captain.

Specialists within the team were able to aid preparation for matches as ex-Servicemen would offer their services to conduct physical training and in the case of Britain, military officers could help their teams by contributing advice and playing styles that they had picked up in Asia and Africa whilst serving in the Army. Hockey effectively had no real professional component to the game in Europe at all.

Turning to other parallel sports was of little use either as Rugby, Rowing and Racquet sports were all stuck in the same vein. Football, however, was not. English football in the two decades since the end of World War II was prospering with huge crowds, player wage increases and gaining ground in the European and world arena. That was at the macro level, but locally in professional clubs, Managers were employing full time coaches who were making a big difference.

Most sporting pundits will have known Joe Mercer as Manager of Manchester City, but the person who was really responsible for the club's rise in the 1960's was his Assistant, Malcolm Allison. The same applied with future England Manager Ron Greenwood at West Ham and indeed with the coaches at Liverpool F.C. in Bill Shankly's Boot Room.

Not only at club level was this expansion in technical guidance more prominent, but also within the corridors of the Football Association itself. For some considerable time, the F.A. had appointed a Coaching Director to oversee operations, establish a hierarchy of coaching qualifications and to steer the nation's future players in a controlled direction. Walter Winterbottom throughout these years leading up to 1970 had been a football pioneer in recognising the virtues and value of having a Team Coach at every level of play.

Yet, he wanted a 'badged' team coach. His efforts quietly continued in the shadows of the Alf Ramsey era of national team success which had culminated in the winning of the World Cup in 1966. Without doubt, football had created direct lines of development between junior park football and the scout's role in talent identification, which heralded the journey of young players towards the professional (or top Amateur) teams. They, in turn, took over the young player in his teenage years, offering 'B' team (schoolboy) 'A' team (Apprentice professional) competitive and coached football into the mainstream of the senior game.

Still, more to the point, had hockey done the same? Sadly, there was no fusion between the two sports. Both viewed each other with either suspicion from the hockey side to outright derision from the football end. Yes, it was undoubtedly a class thing, blue collar pitched against white collar. Despite many common similarities they never would intend to overlap and learn from each other. Accidentally though, there were common threads that meant that hockey would, as it were, come to the coaching party. It was inevitable that the governing body of Hockey, the H.A. Council would have noticed football's success in these years and its undying popularity with the public. Hockey was insular, it had not yet opened up the British version of the game to real competition at club or international level with its European counterparts.

Football, on the other hand, had been pushing into Europe for well over a decade with European Cup success for major British clubs like Manchester United, Tottenham Hotspur and Celtic, all winning major trophies. By 1970, hockey was light years behind football in Britain, and with no World Cup competition at the top end, no leagues to speak of internally either, and precious little development at junior level to note, something had to change.

It had to and it did! Many ex-National Servicemen in Britain had become very motivated to take up careers in physical education, teaching and sport in general. It was this generation that were genuinely interested in going on to College and University to learn more about the theory side of sport that they had essentially practiced whilst experiencing National Service. There were those that gravitated directly into teaching, but a major sector looked to a potential mecca for sports development. That mecca from humble beginnings as a four part fragmented entity, was to grow into the educational establishment that would dominate all things sporting right up to today.

It was Loughborough Colleges, note the title. It consisted of Colleges, split into engineering science, art, handicrafts, and sport. These Colleges would metamorphose into the Loughborough University that was to be formed in the later 1970's. The site, central to all parts of England, could and would be specialist in nature, and its aim was to offer excellence in any of its disciplines and to prepare its students to impart that level of knowledge as they prepared to be teachers in schools and higher education across Britain. Loughborough literally was setting a fast pace and by 1970 was already challenging the 'old boys' stranglehold of Oxford and Cambridge in sporting excellence and performance.

The essential difference between these systems was simple –Loughborough was educating students to teach, but it was also teaching them their game of their particular interest, and ensuring that what they knew was in a solid overall physical education framework. Loughborough was practical and relevant, Oxbridge was talented but becoming a place of assumed Elitism. The teachers at Loughborough had experienced competition themselves and were more likely to have been educated in the school of hard knocks. Their students did not meet the barriers of strict academia and were able to progress uninterrupted from schoolboy success to recipients of a BSc with honours in Physical Education, later to be transformed to Sports Science.

John Cadman

One such budding student who entered Loughborough along such a prescribed cause was a young John Cadman in the mid fifties. John was to become the man to transform coaching in the United Kingdom as an organised priority for hockey. More than any other subsequent figure in the game, he was to become the rallying point around which all future coaching standards, awards and procedures would be related to in the development of hockey in the ensuing decades.

Before John was appointed as National Coach in 1970, it is essential to note both here and anywhere else in the world there was no such post as a Coaching Director. He was the first of his kind. Not the Coach to the National team, but a position set out to guide the direction of the game for the nation, in this case England.

His road and background are well worth studying for all young embryo coaches out there. He entered Loughborough having left the family business in auctioneering and surveying as a talented cricket and football player. He was already a member of the Essex Cricket 2nd team as a youngster and his explosive speed and power had enabled him to excel at his Friends School in Saffron Walden and during his National Service days in both sports.

At Loughborough in his second year, he was approached by the captain of hockey to give the sport a try as he seemed a bit disillusioned by football. John takes up the story,

"I felt I needed a new challenge at the age of 20, and was approached by this hockey rep called Sutcliffe. I had never played the game of Hockey and was clueless. He placed me at right-half emphasising, 'to run like I did at football and when given the ball, to play cricket with it!!'"

Unconventional advice indeed, but John took to the game like a duck to water and within months was in the Loughborough Colleges First Team and playing for Leicestershire. His career continued having graduated from University, with Beckenham, probably one of the top three clubs in the nation and very much influenced by an ex-Cambridge and Scotland player, Bill Vans Agnew. Here, of all ironies, was the ultimate in two team mates, one to become as an establishment Oxbridge man, the Great Britain Coach in 1972 and the other to rise through the ranks to be England's First National Coach in 1970.

Coaching, certainly in Britain, as an organised and professional pursuit, could well be claimed to have been born here in the far reaches of South-East London at one of the country's premier clubs, and do not forget, all the two icons played were friendlies in a very comfy, cosy social framework of London club hockey.

These were early days for coaching, but one must wonder what the professional relationship was like between Bill and John both at Beckenham as players in the late 50's and then again as Coaches and indeed Managers of the National game when true coaching took hold during the period this book is detailed to assess. One thing was sure, and that was that Beckenham was a particularly successful club team in this era where the midfield expertise of Vans Agnew and the direct pace and power of the wide and centre forward abilities of Cadman were too much for many opponents.

John Cadman played 25 times for England and Great Britain (probably equivalent to 100 Tests today) and competed at the Tokyo Olympic Games

70

under Manager Robin Fletcher and Assistant Roger Tattershall. In describing his international experience, where Britain had finished 8th at the Games, John outlined that coaching as we know it today was not in evidence, but there was no lack of structured advice from senior pros in a team whose average age was 28!

I asked him about the composition of the squad,

"It was commonplace to have older teams then notably in Britain as many of us having completed National Service and University, were 23 or 24 before settling with a Club. Though there were always major contributions in numbers from Oxbridge, the squad was still very well balanced, seldom was there any "us and them" attitude in the group. We were talented, but not internationally aware enough of how other nations were playing and progressing. The tactical element hardly existed with us, it was purely a game of technical skill and that belonged almost exclusively to the Indians and Pakistan's of our era"

John retired from teaching and moved back to the family business in East Anglia, still playing regular club hockey for Bury St Edmunds, but at the age of 31, he knew his International days as a striker were numbered. Even though he was out of education, he very much retained his teaching skills and his knowledge accrued over the previous decade at every level.

By the end of the 60's, the Hockey Association were waking up after what was really two also-ran appearances at the Tokyo and Mexico City Olympics, averaging only a 7th place. In simple terms, Australasian, Asia and African nations had overtaken the mother country as well as the competitive continental nations of Holland, Spain and Germany. The new era was soon to bring about greater awareness of the game with the FIH introducing a bi-annual World Cup to be added to the recent European Cup of Nations in the late 60's.

The Council of England Hockey would take the football coaching model and advertise for 1970 the post of National Coach. They had the year previously selected 15 senior coaches to impact their philosophy on the game, but what was that? England exhibited a diverse coverage of views and slants on the game across the country.

It was left to two Loughborough hockey men to apply for the job, Stan Wigmore, already a physical education lecturer , and the young 35 year old upstart ex-student, John Cadman! Evidently, when Stan was interviewed, he informed the Council Executive the man they were looking for was waiting outside to be interviewed next!

Cadman became the first National Coach and by our defining year of 1972, had established a Technical Development Plan for Coaches and Coaching. First, he had to meet the problems that he was to confront to push England coaching to the fore.

"We needed to establish our own Hockey Association Coaching Scheme. At the time, we had only 90 hockey coaches registered in the country and required a tiered hierarchy to be introduced. Coaching was perceived by many purely as a means to imparting skills, we needed to go a lot further than that to encompass models of physical and tactical component coaching. To my mind, we started with no junior development, little coaching in state schools, no competitive adult leagues and clearly not nearly enough qualified coaches in clubs or schools"

John had seen the necessity to breakdown the old "hockey in winter, cricket in summer" beer clubs that were inhibiting youth from being attracted to the sport. As highlighted in an earlier chapter, the club was merely in many cases a hub for social activity rather than a centre to develop the game with unashamed competition. It was almost as bad in the state schools where the great majority of physical educationalists on the male side of the game had never been schooled in hockey. It was not much more advanced in girls' schools where antiquated attitudes towards hockey prevailed across the board.

The new post allowed John to take the game to the people, to throw forward pilot schemes for Sunday youth development, to introduce small team Indoor Hockey in the winters and most of all, to outline a curriculum for grading coaches. With the help from a sponsor, "Green Shield Stamps", he was able to offer coaching courses for teachers and an increasing number of club personnel directed at men and women. Whether on a weekly basis during the season at set centres or at what was to become the most popular move of all, at summer weekly residential courses, Cadman worked his magic, and by 1985, fifteen years on, he had 2000 coaches qualified in England alone, a twenty fold increase from his starting point.

The atmosphere changed, leagues all-round the country were springing up within months of Cadman's appointment with indoor tournaments at the Crystal Palace and regular televised Internationals from Wembley and Lords. Hockey was expanding under a coaching umbrella.

It was not an easy transition for the old guard as more and more children and women were beginning to invade the clubhouse and progressively through the decade invade the inner sanctuary of British hockey's establishment. One of the by-products of the coaching revolution was in Britain, for the first time, to see women at coaching courses run by the men's "Hockey Association" deserting their trusted "All England Women's Hockey Association".

These courses were fun! A whole week in July or August spent at a Country House, known as Bisham Abbey or Lilleshall under the guidance of John Cadman and soon to join him as Assistant National Coach, Trevor Clarke. The author knows this because he attended one such course at the tender age of 21!! The days were structured as teachers and embryo coaches from all over England and the World were taught hockey, the Cadman way. The base skills and exercises were followed by practices in grids, then onto small team games. Each component was a building block to move onto the next technical level. Coaching notes were supplied to help prioritise the course attendant's knowledge and application.

Notably, the teachers were taught the intricacies of the game, and we players were taught how to teach and import the skills. On the final two days, we were firstly internally tested as part of the course, then externally assessed by an independent examiner to whether we reached a Preliminary Coaching Certificate (PCC) or an H.A.2 badge or the converted H.A.1

Whatever happened at our test results, these courses attracted over 50 attendees per week and the hockey and social interaction was unparalleled. Anyone attending would have learned even more from that dimension alone as course members came from as far afield as Holland, Zambia and Canada, and at all levels of coaching and teaching. The facilities at the two principal centres augmented the quality of the Senior Coaches as top class hockey facilities lay beside the residential and social blocks on offer.

Yet, you were left with an over-riding impression of organisation and quality from the new National Coaches Seminar courses. Yes, it was fun, but you departed with a written qualification to hand, eager to go out and impart the broad circulation you had been surrounded by for seven days. Cadman had pushed at his vision, but more than this, he had been prepared to demonstrate master coaching sessions himself during the course.

His theoretical background was always very well researched, but it was his delivery as a coach to the group that was extra special. He was clear as crystal, uncomplicated, structured and always player-friendly. He undertook his model sessions as a phased progression, always stressing the vital areas of a practice and its relationship to the bigger game.

As a course member myself, just one aspect almost dwarfed the rest in respect to John. It was his voice and the integrity that he stood for in his communication to fellow coaches. The voice was an Essex tilt on a London accent, precise but detailed at the same time with a definite pitch on it when accentuating a point. It was easy to be a pupil of John F. Cadman Esquire and many more across the globe from India to Canada would experience his control of the coaching medium.

He had brought all this to England in 1970 and in the next 15 years he had built up coaching numbers, a coaching hierarchy, but most of all, a coaching quality that was well respected across the globe as a model for countless countries to adopt.

Later in his coaching life, John enjoyed coaching coaches and took up near on a coaching residency at Cambridge University. During his career, he had only coached three senior international matches, unbeaten he is at pains to point out, when filling in for an England team crisis in 1981. During his time, the immediate pre-AstroTurf era was intertwined with the later years of the Amateur code. Yet, this made little difference to John's interpretation of the game of hockey, always staying true to his original principle of coaching essential basic skills in a team tactical format. He never really was influenced by overseas trends and developments, but very much brought the game home in an English context to both players and coaches.

His was very much the internal interpretation of the game to those eager to learn more. Yes, indeed as our previous dynamics from the USA in terms of technology were being unleashed onto this flooded market of coaches, it was ultimately a hand in glove situation. John Cadman had provided the framework and numbers for coaching in England, and this was soon to be expanded not only by the technological assets of synthetic turf and video analysis, but by a new breed of coaches and coaching.

If John Cadman had secured the vital components that made up a national hockey programme, it was Horst Wein who literally pushed at the boundaries of the sport. Both men had run a parallel background with Horst playing a similar number of international test matches as a wide right-wing striker during the same period that John had played at the Olympics in 1964. The two of them were physical educationalists and the same trait of a desire to improve and expand the game's thinking was the essential part of their professional lives.

Horst Wein

Horst Wein displayed one extra quality right from the start. He saw hockey as a global entity. For him, hockey, like football, belonged to the world and he regarded his place as right at its epicentre. He genuinely viewed his role in hockey as emanating new ideas, continually drawing from his experiences in hockey and all other sports. Whereas Cadman was national, Wein was very international.

Germany, as it was then, West Germany, had never really achieved in the medal stakes as a hockey nation, but in being awarded the big prize in 1972, it made an interesting appointment in asking Horst to be the chief organiser of the hockey tournament at the Munich Games. The fact that these papers selected 1972 as the breakthrough year in the modern development of hockey was no accident. Not only at that stage had Horst Wein taken up a very influential role in setting the stage for Munich's hockey success as a competition but also the host nation shocked the world by winning Olympic Gold. Horst had set the climate into which the Germans had gleefully followed. It is very much worth noting the detail of his academic contribution to the sport first of all. His inaugural work, 'The Science of Hockey' gave the game away in terms of how he saw the hockey world and beyond as early as the mid 1970's.

"This relationship between training and competition, used in conjunction with the latest knowledge derived from a scientific approach to the sport should determine the development of any game. It has done so in the majority of Olympic sports, but hardly so in hockey. This sport in the last few years had developed rapidly in some parts of the world but the evidence of the 70's decade has suggested that this knowledge has passed largely unrecorded"

In these statements he demonstrated pointedly the underdevelopment within the game of hockey and notably implied how stagnation had gripped the English speaking part of the hockey world. These words inevitably angered many of the so called authorities of the game who clearly were destabilised by such a factual challenge to the ways of the status quo. From 1973 Horst was to spread his wings by leaving Germany to take up the National Coach position for Spain, a position he held for ten years. Again, Spain had never really disturbed the medals board until they themselves had hosted the inaugural World Cup in 1971 in Barcelona with a silver medal.

Horst had arrived in Spain to be very much welcomed, but also to be carefully monitored and reviewed throughout his time there. The sport of hockey in Spain whether in the capital Madrid or out in Catalonia was dominated by the interest of rich powerful sports and social clubs. Simply put, hockey was played by the economic elite, the upper echelon of Spanish society. How would they take to a down to earth physical educationalist like Horst, and a foreign one at that?

Indeed, though he had involved himself with tournament organisation, the authoring of books on hockey and lecture series even at this stage around the world, Horst Wein was the practical hockey coach. He was to develop in Barcelona during these years as a Master Coach and Spain was to be his pupil. Don't let anyone tell you otherwise, even those doyens of establishment hockey at the Polo Club in Barcelona nor Club Egara in Terrassa or even the Club de Campo in well-heeled Madrid.

National Club interests were paramount during these early years after 1972 with the internal championships of the country vital to the game's well being in Spain. Clubs were measured by their men's hockey success and considerable amounts of membership monies and donations were ploughed into hosting prestigious tournaments in hockey, tennis, and polo. Though Germany had its fair share of top facilities at clubs and a competitive Bundesliga in indoor and outdoor hockey, it was nothing to be compared to the wealth of the game in Spain.

Horst Wein had to tread very gingerly as his bosses were powerful men in and out of hockey. Yet he was motivated and self-inspired, remember that comment, "This knowledge has passed largely unrecorded," reflected Horst's inner frustration that hockey people, as nice and genuine as they were, had missed the boat in terms of physical, technical, and tactical development on a worldwide scale.

Here lay the seeds of Wein's eventual future in the larger, more competitive game of football. Did he show any parallel interest in the bigger ball game at this stage?

There was no evidence to that, but you have to wonder during these years in the 70's and early 80's, was it a coincidence that he chose to settle in one of the worlds greatest football cities, Barcelona. It is beyond belief that there was no cross fusion of ideas and training methods between the Nou Camp and the Royal Spanish Hockey Federation! I can't believe anything other than that Horst was a regular visitor to F.C. Barcelona at this time.

Yes, the history books of this decade show Spain winning the European Cup of Nations in 1974 and also claiming gold at a partially attended Olympics in 1980, and being a regular team at the early Champions Trophy events in Pakistan. Their brand of hockey was different and notably shadowed the emphasis that Horst had placed as the new priorities for the game, whether it was to be played on the new Astroturfs or on the soon to be forgotten natural grass fields.

As a student of the game, everything he approached was well researched, not really surprising as his professional life in these years was based around the centres of learning in Universities. Yet there was a sure footed function about the way he presented his coaching and training of teams. Comparing him to the big brother sport of football, he was not an inspirational icon like Brian Clough, nor a superb training ground communicator like Terry Venables. Horst Wein's contribution to hockey was as an ideas man based on a strong hockey intellect, a coach who pushed at the edges and defined new ways of presenting the game both technically and tactically. His was a world sans frontieres in sport, and he an innovator whose challenges and ideas motivated many to enter the coaching ranks. To my own personal amusement, he infuriated hockey's ruling powers and like many before and after him, those same power brokers were fearful of his knowledge and experience.

To be specific, let's take a closer look at what Horst brought to the table as the father of systemised coaching. The majority of his academic work still rotated around the base technical skills and how they should be methodically coached. His approach was to break down the skill in a stage by stage analysis through the art of coaching demonstration. He directed the player to look at differing angles during the demonstration at the potential pitfalls in the execution of a skill. He emphasised an interesting point, to many a coach's relief, that any demonstration ought to be shown slowly and that verbal explanation must follow the practical demonstration.

He strongly believed that the coach must separate the physical display which was directed at the eyes of the class from the verbal explanation which concentrates on the ears of the group. Eyes plus ears, he contended, equalled the complete understanding of the player. His progressions would move into shadow play without opponents or time or space constraints, then finally into a competitive framework with opponents. Horst greatly believed in a variety of imaginative small team games which would stimulate the player's mutual enjoyment and understanding of the topic involved.

When applying this model to positional acumen on the field, he could be typified by his consistency of approach with a quote on the success of right wing play,

"A winger who relies solely on his speed and solid technique, but is a stranger to the idea of playing off the ball, is less valuable therefore, in the modern game ,than a player whose every attack reveals his deep understanding of the game."

What took the eye with Horst Wein was his tackling of topics then regarded as on the periphery of the game, and still today in 2015, are not fully grasped by the majority of schools and club coaches all around the hockey world. I particularly was at home with, and motivated by his attention to detail on areas of the game like the running style of players, the counter attack, variation of tactical systems of play, movement off the ball and the role of passing switch plays in hockey.

Even today great hordes of players run without the ball with sticks representing a horizontal barrier to forward fast propulsion. It defies belief that generations of female players in particular are or have been trapped inside the hockey stick barrier, rather than with a strong right hand grip halfway down the stick to bring the left hand to connect when in possession. Horst correctly suggested this was the first restriction to a player's acquiring stick skills and athletic movement on the field of play.

Indeed, with the stick head leading very much to the open side, there is no doubt that it accentuated the dominance of right hand side skills and play as it would involve quite some manoeuvring to get any stick positioning from that extreme right to the left reverse stick zone. This would also explain the Europeans' tendency to move the whole body around to field a ball on their left hand side rather than using quick hand speed to turn the stick head over to trap the ball.

If our sticks only point one way, then it naturally follows that the team will face that way too. Hence, the obsession for many in the last five decades with the open stick's role in developing strong but limited skill. In many teams from juniors in schools, clubs, to full national and international level, players have been discarded because they have displayed an array of technical skills on both sides of their stick and body.

Horst recognised the fallacy of the theme of possession. How many times have coaches vented frustration at having had the lion's share of possession only to lose the game by the narrowest of margins. It is of course what, where, how and when that really matters when it comes to possession, and it was here on reading any of Wein's works that you could identify his systematic approach to the first pass out of defence and its importance of accuracy and direction in establishing position at the next stage.

Understanding that many top level tournaments are played at temperatures over 23°C containing as many as seven matches in ten days, Horst knew the attacking emphasis of wholehearted effort and interplay of all the ten field players was an exhaustive business, notably in the days before unlimited substitution. His match play strategies were commonly based on absorbing opposing attacks that had dominated possession, but possession inside the field on his terms and at his team's enforced tempo. The job slowing down an opponent's movement, dispossessing in a favourable area, only then to strike quickly with limited numbers but in greater space, was covered as an integral part of his "Science of Hockey".

Spain's tactical progression throughout his period there was testament to his unique grasp of how to perform the counter attack in hockey with limited team possession of the ball in the game. An early education for this author was indeed observing his Spanish squad's play against Asian and Australasian teams in hot and humid conditions as they challenged bigger nations with often superior physical and technical assets.

His selection of organised defenders, visual early passing midfielders with highly mobile interchangeable strikers showed such parallels with Spanish football. It was a classic case of a coach assessing the assets of his players and utilising them to the full. Moreover, it was not dull hockey as his front and middle lines were set to play with such fluidity. I would like to repeat that his teams set the trend for a generation, but a succession of players and teams anywhere in the world were never to be content or patient enough to operate off 30-40% possession in a game. Too many thought if they had not reached 70% possession, then they were not in control of a match.

Horst Wein was not understood in the main in Asia or Australasia, and after his differences with Hugo Buddinger and the Germans, he was more envied than lauded by the Europeans. Constantly pinpointed as one of those founders of tactical systems of play that broke away from the orthodox five: three: two pyramid formation, he fielded a great deal of criticism from inflexible thinkers on the game. His reliance on strict man to man defensive and middle field marking had often put the shackles on opposing players of technical talent but tactical naivety. His coaching opponents now had to think how to deal with a host of tactical challenges and many of them were simply ill-equipped to respond because of their intransigence and conformity to familiar and comfortable patterns played in their countries.

79

Soon he was experimenting with presses in various parts of the field and the use of attacking functions from defenders originally set as deep players on the field. This of course brought a newly found mobility to hockey players right across the pitch. When you looked at a Spanish team, it was very difficult to discern which of them played in which position. In observing Pakistan, Australia, New Zealand, England, Malaysia, or India, positional specialisation did mean the stereotyping of positions according to the size of the individuals. The tall, leggy, long reach individuals were placed in the back positions, while strikers appeared clearly as faster, slimmer players with speed and agility to the fore.

Spanish and Argentinian hockey personnel were all round players with a much more uniform posture which incorporated all the physical elements in any one player. Thus, it was much easier for coaches like Horst to select more fluid and adaptable team players that could perform a variety of tactical functions. Not just Spain but Argentina remained a competitive force in top club and international hockey for decades to come despite their paucity in numbers, and this fact was to a large extent attributable to Horst Wein's tenure in Spain up until November 1983.

Our two highlighted coaches, both former international forwards and physical educational specialists, had introduced and mastered a systematic approach to national and international coaching that had never been witnessed before. They had established a template for others to follow and extend. Their work over these two decades had achieved acclaim by their academic and practical emphasis and was to inspire a new generation of teachers and coaches of the game of hockey. John and Horst had indeed opened the door, notably in Europe, to the art and science of coaching. Now it was to be the turn of coaches to expand where we were to coach, and the answer to that was firmly placed in institutions, all ready and willing to comply. It was at the Hockey Clubs.

Horst Wein's "The Science of Hockey"; the first modern technical and tactical work and "Games for Hockey Training" by John Cadman

-Part F-

SuperClubs

European clubs were ready to enlarge and prosper with the added intent of available competition and achievement. Now in the 1970's they could not only compete with their rivals within their own borders, but for the first time they could contest a European club championship. Running parallel to their football equivalents, the champion club teams were those that pioneered the best facilities, keen organisation, and adhered to the new coaching trends of the day.

Names like Klein Switzerland, Swartz -Weiss Koln, Southgate, Royal Leopold and the Real Club de Polo Barcelona were all sumptuously named, but they were also all well funded by club members who had made their millions in post-war boom times. It was not only a question of players being subsidised by these urban giants, they were also guaranteed direct access into the world of international hockey. To qualify for 'Europe', it was a pre-condition to win your National Qualifying League or Cup, and with that incentive, new clubs appeared on the horizon to challenge the old order.

Club hockey originated in its original form in the South-West suburbs of London in the second half of the 19th century, but soon the game had spread to all parts of the British Empire. Yet, Surbiton and Teddington never featured in those Euro contests, whilst unlikely names like Klein Switzerland and Polo Club, Barcelona were an annual fixture. How did a Polo Club from the Latin world achieve such notoriety and present such a tradition that went back to the beginning of the 20th century?

Real Club de Polo existed as early as 1897 when a group of well-heeled gentleman would assemble in the Restaurant de Francia in a fashionable Barcelona boulevard. They were a social mix that networked through their businesses and marriage in high society. It was just not enough for them to shoot the breeze together, as they wanted more, and on realising they all shared a common interest in horses, they decided to found a recreation club to further their interests in what would be known as the University zone close to the future site of the Polo Club. This type of meeting of social friends was in itself very commonplace throughout Europe as the basis of establishing sports clubs.

So, the traditional club model was there in Barcelona at the turn of the century, but why, then, Polo in Spain? After all, it was the British that had discovered the Sport of Kings out in India, the competitive origins of which were played amongst the Maharajas and the highest ranks of the British colonial army. There is some debate on how Polo and even subsequently, how hockey arrived in Barcelona. Was it purely British equestrian personnel that had taken vacation time in the area to pass on the sport of Polo that had come back to England via the military? More likely it seems that it was a more circuitous route via Argentina.

With Spanish settlement in and around the Buenos Aires province in the last decade of the 19th century, there would have been witnessed the flow of British migrants sent out to build the railways into the interior from the staging port city to export beef to the homeland. Large sporting clubs were introduced among the ex-patriot population in the 1870's who spent their leisure time playing an organised version of Football, Hockey and Polo. Any modern observer would see the parallels in the layout and exclusiveness of clubs like Hurlingham in Buenos Aires to how Polo Club has presented itself in Barcelona.

Surely with migration running in both directions, it was very conceivable that the Polo Club in Barcelona had roots in Argentina and Colonial Britain. Hockey, in turn, in the early twentieth century had become part of the club boasting one team, but importantly at this stage, it was not a Section of the club. Towards 1912, Espanyol stood as the only club to have that special status in the Catalan region.

Polo's hockey team pulled together and trained outside of the club in a newly built ice rink! This contributed towards them acquiring official status, but what they needed to do was to issue a challenge to Espanyol on the pitch. To everyone's surprise and delight, Polo defeated its rivals by five goals to two. So important was this result that the players then could produce a petition to be considered as a Section of the club.

Rightfully accepted, by the end of 1913, the club produced two teams amidst growing excitement. This over-enthusiasm ironically led to such internal friction between the teams that they had to be given separate training times at the local ice rink where there was further antagonism from the skating fraternity who resented their ice rink being taken over by these new hockey invasions. Out of such chaos and internal strife came a sense of order and administration in the form of Manuel Nogareda. Rather than join the melee of the hockey games, he stood back and umpired the encounters, and was taken to write up the critical reports of matches after the post game socials had died down.

These were regularly attended by the more aristocratic part of Catalan society and soon hockey became very much part of the social calendar along with equestrian events at the club. This reinforced the hockey Section's credibility and influence. As Jose Miguel Casades was to write in 1915 in the specialised magazine, 'Stadium':

"Fortunately a new initiative awoke the passion for hockey within some distinguished sportsmen of the aristocratic society of the Real Club de Polo of Barcelona. They train regularly in its splendid fields – certain that it is the only society in Barcelona that plays hockey in suitable conditions at present. And they do not only play amongst themselves but also active advertising resulted in other teams being interested in playing them. This is the case of Club Deportivo Espanyol, against which they played a friendly game as a response to their demands. Good impressions are also perceived from the city of Terrassa and it is likely that a team from this city will soon play the Polo team. Lastly it is worth mentioning that the Sportiva Pompeya society – this important entity is always interested in supporting any initiative that helps promoting the sport in any of its forms – has also created its hockey section."

How appropriate, even a century ago, that it was recorded that the sport of hockey was spreading to the nearby city of Terrassa. Soon after Polo Club's emergence, it was to influence indirectly the expansion to such clubs as Egara and Athletico Terrassa which later along with F.C. Barcelona would form a quartet of competition that would extend well through the centenary recently celebrated.

Polo Club retained its sporting dominance for the next fifty years with an expansion of equestrian Gymkanas and a direct connection into the Spanish Olympic federation by hosting a range of show jumping events at the club. Luckily it was not affected by either World War and it was not really until the Olympic cycles got underway in the 1950's that hockey emerged for its first phase of success.

It has been noted how the club had acted as a substantial forum for networking amongst the upper classes. Barcelona still stood as the more industrialised city of Spain with a very well developed banking and commercial sector with close ties to France. With such activity there was created a whole range of family connections with great members of these families who would meet to discuss business at the weekends at the club.

Such families would have included names that would become legends in the playing and administration of the sport in Spain and at world level. When asked about Polo notoriety in hockey, one is inclined to just look at names of individuals like Amat, Fabregas, Deo, and Calzado rather than team supremacy at any level. The most influential of this group was Juan Angle Calzado, a man that rose as a junior player for Polo to become an Olympic silver medalist to the ultimate as President of the F.I.H. between 1996 and 2001. Talk Polo Club, think Juan Calzado.

Throughout the 50's, this elegant player witnessed the post war changes as the Polo Club's hockey section opened its doors to promote the sport. Calzado was very much part of the drive to internationalise, as Polo first invited Parisian hockey clubs to Barcelona. Juan Angel later admitted that part of the reason for this was to seek a reciprocal arrangement whereby the French would return the invitation. Evidently several of the Catalan players wanted out of Franco's dictatorship and sporting trips were one of the few ways to achieve this end.

The trouble was that these players just required a one-way ticket!! More and more teams visited Polo both from outside of Spain, and inside the country from teams like Joleseta on the Atlantic coast and Club de Campo in Madrid. It was the latter that guested at the Polo Club in the first fully televised hockey game shot in black and white between the two clubs in 1957.

Prior to this, what is known today as the Three Kings Tournament had been introduced as the oldest club tournament in the world. It was unlike the very old English festivals that had no winner, just a series of matches.

Still, Calzado the Olympian had caught the spirit of the age with this January tournament. He had always stated that the Barcelona venue would stress the essential nature of friends in hockey across the borders. From the start in 1948 through to today, there has always been an emphasis on youth as boys and girls attended from as far afield as Holland and Germany, Ireland and England, France and Italy to compete and enjoy the compatibility of the sport in a friendly setting (see poster from 1972).

It was an honour and a privilege for you to be invited by the famous son of Real Club de Polo, Juan Calzado, whether you were a school, a University or a European club champion. Without a doubt there was a status to any club that could host international teams of such a magnitude that arrived to play in Barcelona. The city provided the perfect backdrop with its clear and sunny climate in January. More and more clubs would be queuing up to participate as the four day tournament was a perfect release from harsh Northern European winter conditions.

The tournament gained prestige by offering the best in on and off the field facilities as, in time, grass was replaced by redgra, which in turn gave way to three state of the art Astroturfs. Yet it was technology and the hockey dynamic of competitive match play that gradually pushed the Three Kings Tournament into a less popular proposition by the end of the century. Cheap airfares to go further afield, and the selection of so many National team players to abide by their training schedules, have meant that there has been less of a high powered performance edge to the tournament of late.

However, even now in 2015, Junior National teams and club sides from Holland, Belgium, England, Italy and France make up the competitors that still enjoy the traditional friendly welcome which is part and parcel of the clubs ethos. Even the young umpires at the tournament are closely mentored with experienced old hands looking after a pool of hopeful ambitious young officials. Such seemed to be the case in 1972 when a 16 year old confident youngster umpired at all of the junior tournament matches including the 'final' big match between Real Club de Polo and an English hockey school from the London area, Kingston Grammar School.

His name was Santiago Deo, who ventured forth to spend a life time umpiring well over 300 Senior International test matches, a true phenomenon for a Spaniard who recently has put his name forward for election to the Presidency of the Spanish Hockey Federation. His rise to fame was almost Churchillian with Santi's shared indulgence of the Havana variety, the Cuban cigar!!

Club de Polo can celebrate the fabulous father and son duo of Juan and then Pol Amat, although the latter of F.I.H player of the year notoriety, had migrated to play in Terrassa. Both had the distinction of winning World Cup Silver medals, as did the Fabregas brothers in the First Inaugural World Cup. Where was it held? At the Polo Club, where else?

The club has never really compromised on its image as it has always represented the traditional ethics of the game as its raison d'etre. It would continue to live up to the motto, "one city, one club", and excel in hosting events like International Show Jumping and then in 1992, the Olympic Games Qualifier for hockey. It still remains one of the grandest hockey clubs in the world, seldom to be influenced by the neighbouring Nou Camp of F.C. Barcelona with all of its glitter and sporting ambitions.

Real Club de Polo stands tall in its proud history and heritage, seemingly oblivious to the new brand of hockey club which was hell bent in winning, and winning trophies all over the world. We will have to turn to a tiny village in a small country to discover that club story.

Part Two

The social fabric of European club hockey was thus firmly established in centres like Barcelona, Madrid, Berlin, and London. True, but what about the aspirations of the continent's smallest country, the Netherlands? Clubs like Bloemendaal, Amsterdam, and Kampong Utrecht were founded as early as 1891.

So, how was it that a small family based club like Bloemendaal in less than thirty years could lay claim to being the top club team in the world? The circumstances which pushed this village club into the limelight were not unique. Indeed, they were commonly shared by a host of Dutch teams over the very same period.

As Europe grew and prospered, so did the industrial giants and bankers of the Netherlands economy. Wealth had come to many parts of the country which acted as the perfect go-between of its larger, more powerful neighbours Germany, Britain and France.

Even down to language skills, the Dutch middle-upper class produced a number of managers of multi-linguists based in multinational companies. Technology was highlighted here as a means to national prosperity with Phillips, Royal Dutch Shell, and leading Dutch banking concerns like Rabobank at the forefront of European Community success.

The human resources element was equally transferred to the way the Dutch handled their leisure time. Hockey clubs vastly increased their numbers, expanded their financial resources, and took pride in building synthetic turf facilities in plentiful numbers across the country. The head personnel in clubs and at the international level really came to a classic accommodation. They created an emphasis to highlight the development of the game at youth level at one end of the spectrum whilst expecting nothing but international medal success at the top end.

It was the perfect sandwich. The Dutch dynamic had over the years been attempting to spread the hockey message beyond its shores to other countries, notably in coaching. Those efforts in general have not fully succeeded because even these enterprising Hollanders had underestimated the uniqueness of their hockey product based around their own cultural identity.

There is a natural co-existence on and off the field between the conservative and liberal, and between youth and experience which continually brings energy to the Dutch equation. Talk hockey with any Dutch man or woman and you will need to be passionate about what you say, whatever it is.

Hockey Club Bloemendaal

The club was established in the dormitory village on the outskirts of the prosperous town of Haarlem in the late nineteenth century. It had tasted success at national level throughout its history with a scattering of international players, but was always most well known for the Swiss-style chalet of a clubhouse which was surrounded by herds of cows on one side and of all things, by the Bloemendaal Cricket Club on the other!!

Cricket as a part of an all the year round sporting calendar, social mixing and affinity to a very upper-middle class were the realities that greeted any visitor to the club right up until the early 1980's. The production line of top class players still continued as Doyer, Diepeveen, and Heijn were fixtures in the Netherlands teams of this era. These three like many others had been schooled within the club's youth programme, which at that time had been boosted and expanded with installation of two floodlit synthetic pitches. These national legends had not learnt the sport at school but for a period of ten years had arrived at the club three times per week to receive specific training from their elders up through the club.

The sport was then ready for the interaction of sponsors with the club's grandees utilising their close commercial contacts. The latter were drawn to a sport with huge numbers of young boys and girls, national men's and women's teams that were consistently winning medals at the majors, and noticeably producing figures like Ties Kruize, Tommy Van T'Hek and Lisanne Lejeune who were prominent figures beyond Bloemendaal hockey in the Dutch sporting world.

Bloemendaal's suburbs were affluent, their inhabitants well used to success in their daily lives. Inevitably the hockey dynamic was soon to kick in here to transform the club from a top competitor to a continental champion. For once, one had to look beyond Dutch hockey to the FIH for a pronouncement made in the early 1990's. The world's governing body announced that the sport was not to continue as it had done for a century on purely amateur lines, but professional modes of play, conduct and support systems could be introduced. Hockey had turned the corner, it had put the game up for sale with the marketplace being the pre-determinant of all club, school and international involvement.

Hockey Club Bloemendaal had been given the green light. Before 1993 they respected the amateur code, and therefore held in check remuneration for players and coaches and held at arm's length the demands of short and long term sponsors interests. Suddenly, players were attracted by not just the honour of playing for one of the oldest clubs in Holland, they now could be handsomely rewarded. Coaches of high quality enjoyed the environment previously, now they could savour the fruits associated with full-time careers. In short, the club became a magnet for the best that the Netherlands was producing. Like Australia in this 90's decade, monetary availability was constant, but in Bloemendaal's case it was derived from private enterprise and multiple donations from within the club.

Just a list of the club's sponsors over the last twenty years would be able to reveal AMB-Ambro, Volvo, and Shell alongside a support 'B' sponsor group that in itself could support the needs of most of today's English Premier League Hockey clubs. Bloemendaal was, from this point on, caught on an ever-increasing merry-go-round of attracting better players, championship success and greater sponsorship in supplying more players for a golden era of Dutch dominance in national and international hockey either side of the millennium.

To cope with this situation, the role of coaching, not just with the first team squad but across the age ranges for boys and girls, had to be professionalised with clear objectives and philosophies and the downright hard task of training a club of one thousand members on just two synthetic pitches. Bloemendaal, right through to today, had the dilemma of many clubs situated in over planned and regulated environments, the scourge of planning permission!!

Affluent neighbours with high property values objected to any new pitch building. Some were even members of the club but they were not prepared for the night glare of new floodlights and reverberating sounds from the increasing number of fields. Naturally, the local cows did not have a say in the matter, but they were all part of an environment that was not interested in becoming an eight pitch Hockey Club Rotterdam!!

Hockey continued its success on the field with new heroes like Floris Jan Bovelander and Remco Van Wyck firing in the goals in the Hofklasse. Yet, the club still demanded more in the 21st century as the new Euro Hockey League was introduced with new rules, multiple camera angles and television feeds to nations all over Europe. As the village club headed for continental trophies its club elders were to push the boat out even further.

Now like football today, it was time to hit the world market of players. After all, Oranje-Swart Eindhoven had signed up Jay Stacey and Shabaz Ahmad from Australia and Pakistan respectively. The Dutch clubs had the financial clout behind them. One Bloemendaal committee member relayed the atmosphere of the time,

"We want only the best, our club members expect to see three or four of the world's top players compete here every year for our club, and to blend with our outstanding home-grown talents like Erik Jazet and Teun de Nooijer."

Hence the arrival over the current decade of Jamie Dwyer and Mathew Swann from Australia and Tom Boon from Belgium.

The gladiators or benevolent mercenaries, whichever way you prefer it, had arrived! It was not a case of instant Euro successes, but the 'Romans' in the spectator stands had to witness where their high price of membership was going. Entertainment and status were the twin towers of this progression in the hockey world.

Nevertheless, where did this leave the village club's tradition of looking after and rearing its own talent? Bloemendaal had essentially pioneered the ideal model, an evolutionary climb from 'Swiss Chalet' to one of the great hockey clubs of the world. Yet lurking here in the wings was often the final phase in the staged development of a sports club. If it ignores its own talent base and if it no longer gives the green light for youngsters like de Nooijer and Bovelander to progress early into the first team on a structured learning curve, these types of clubs will have to face the consequences.

Young players have always been impatient to succeed. Just maybe in former times with the lack of mobility and transport links, these same youngsters would have retained their loyalties to the home base. Today in 2015 choice on everything is out there in the western world. An ambitious young teenager must weigh up his options as he may have to leave the more intense coaching alongside international players in training as at

Bloemendaal or take that huge risk to journey to a lesser club in every way, but one which will provide for him or her a first team regular place. After all, is it not essential for an inexperienced player to test the value of his training hours in how he can apply those skills and disciplines to matchplay.

Such was the dilemma when I visited a family caught up in the predicament at Bloemendaal. Playing for the Dutch U18's was just not enough for the club's coaching staff. Coaching contracts had been handed out in the form of full-time salaries to the leading internationals within the squad, with the next 'B' layer reimbursements also allowing the next level of players a decent standard of pay. Overall, those salaries would cover the majority of the club's 20 leading players.

For the student U20 years of age player, they have found it very difficult to break the mould. "Wilhelm", exasperated, just told me,

"I am frustrated here because I have worked very hard on my perceived weaknesses, but how can you replace eight or nine full Internationals? There is a distinct hierarchy at the club, even these top players have it in their contract that they should not be expected to search for and pick up balls in training. Whether intentional or not, it is one rule for them and another one for us on the edge of the same squad. We have to train the lower teams, the younger groups in the club on a regular basis. They may do it once a season. If we have a midseason debrief none of the foreign internationals pitch up, so what is the point of the group discussion?"

"Wilhelm" represents an enormous problem for the future of the indigenous Dutch players, a problem very much highlighted in the Press and in interviews by much respected ex-Olympic gold medalist Jacques Brinkman. More to the point, Jacques is the father to one of these upper aged teenagers at Kampong and has a true hold on the situation. He has publicly shown fears for the future of the National team as well as Club hockey unless strict guidelines and restrictions are put into place sooner rather than later.

With over half the Australian World Cup final team in 2014 having played their club hockey in the Netherlands and overseas, was it really such a surprise when the hospitable Dutch capitulated in the final by six goals to one to their ever grateful friends from Down Under?

Definitely Brinkman has the message loud and clear that whilst huge numbers of Argentinians, Asians, and Australians take advantage of the free movement of players around the world, the Dutch must understand that they will hold the core positions in any starting line-up in Dutch clubs. There is much concern that the Netherlands will not be able to give opportunities in their clubs to the likes of De Nooiyer's and Van T'Hek's of the future. Added to this, will their team cohesion at international level ever be as tight and efficient again?

Indeed whether at Bloemendaal or any other club for that matter, what might happen when the purse strings are tightened or sponsors move into new differing directions? "No problem", you may hear the committee call, "We will turn to our youth numbers."

The trouble is, my Dutch hockey friends, "Wilhelm" and "Lisanne" will have already moved . . . . to another club

Part Three

So Old Europe's clubs were prospering as the hockey forces of interaction reinforced the competitive trends that swept the continent into the 21st century. Put in simple terms, players could now for reimbursement easily cross borders to play at a higher standard close to international level. The borders, so close together, would pull many of the players from Ireland to Russia together in a harmonious Euro hockey haven. Clubs made all this possible.

Was it the same for clubs in even bigger continents? America was different? Hasn't it always been? They had never heard of clubs in a hockey context, just elitist golf or country clubs that offered the rich their leisure time entertainment. There have been invasions of aliens desperately attempting to demonstrate to Americans that in hockey, the club was the focal point to the identity of the sport.

The trouble was that these aliens that came from Holland, Britain, India, Mexico, the Caribbean, Pakistan and Australia all had one thing in common. They were men, and ex-patriot men at that. They clearly had never heard of Constance Applebee and her successive generations of college hockey fanatics. The latter were women, and the last thing they ever needed was a club!

Inbuilt into the American system of the past and the present has been the notion that field hockey was for women, wasn't it? After all, millions of preppie and high school girls were introduced to the world's sport of hockey since Miss Constance had crossed the pond to bring the game to them in the early twentieth century. The only discrepancy was that she forgot to tell her loyal believers that it was men who had invented the sport in its organised form, and had played it for three decades in England before she even boarded her boat.

Thus it was, that when these expats throughout the 20th century suggested that the club environment would do the girls a power of good, they could not believe it when they were met with a very frosty reception.

After all, didn't these more recent intruders understand that there were three divisions of an elite field hockey programme established since the 1970's and that all the State Universities were ploughing huge transfer fees, over in the States known as sporting scholarships, into the sport of field hockey? At an average American State College game, it would be a case of 300,000 lining up against 360,000 dollars in scholarships representing the two female teams.

The academic and confrontationalist met here as one. It was women against men, natives against intruders, and the liberal college educational hierarchy up against big city new ideas. Ironically it was to be a ruling by the Government, Title 9, that was really intended in Sport to help give a greater deal of equity and equality to women to change what was a man's sporting world. Again, the trouble was that it backfired in field hockey where the so called downtrodden minority were MEN!!

Not able to persuade Athletic Directors to allow boys to play field hockey in schools, and definitely unable to ask for any enlightenment from the block of 95% of female collegiate coaches, the male hockey enthusiast had nowhere to run. By the turn of the 21st century, men as players and coaches were still on death row in hockey performance, finance or development. Still highly suspicious of the males' intents, only a few college coaches actually entertained men as junior assistants, and many were very junior in experience.

Our story is set against such rigidity and perhaps exceeds the development of Real Club de Polo and Bloemendaal in terms of a club that made it to the top in the most dynamic manner, literally from rags to riches. By 2015 this phenomenon had established itself as the biggest and most successful hockey club in North America.

WC Eagles Field Hockey Club

Ever heard what happened when an International hockey umpire met a Chinese junior soccer star who was introduced to a former Philadelphia rock drummer who knew an extended family of Amish? Well, the answer in this twenty-first century is, the WC Eagles FHC.

Jun Kentwell, born Zhang Jun, was handpicked early as a sporting protégé. That was the Chinese way which groomed outstanding talent and nurtured it to maturity to represent the mother country. In Jun's case it was for soccer at the Sports Academy, but soon she was as a teenager to be transferred to the Sports School in Beijing to follow a career in hockey. Hockey in the 1980's was a new pursuit for China with her early coaches moving as master teachers from the sport of Handball at Beijing University.

In effect, only two provinces at that stage were playing hockey, Mongolia and Jiangxi, but bit by bit, enthusiastic young Chinese women became exposed to migrant Indian and Pakistani coaches and by 1988, with the advent of the Seoul Olympics, Korea wielded an important influence in the growth of the game in China. It really acted as the big sister in China's early development, providing tournament opportunities and making accessible the new playing surfaces of Astroturf throughout the next decade.

Jun thrived in a competitive environment where twice daily hockey sessions were augmented by strenuous training runs where literally only the fittest survived. To gravitate towards the National teams, there was no monetary reward, just the satisfaction of becoming a top sportswoman representing the most populous country in the world. Her early environment moulded her beliefs, and bred an inbuilt toughness to regarding hockey and sport as the major priority in her life.

Richard Kentwell very much was the product of the traditional British hockey background growing from school, to club, to county and eventually to junior International level in the 1960's. His subsequent move early in the next decade to the United States displayed his propensity for risk and his desire to move on in life. He would never in his entire career stand still and hang around on projects that were going nowhere. Travelling through the American college coaching system, he found his true niche in hockey when he emerged to become a double Olympic hockey umpire. When this was over he pioneered and expanded the role of Umpires Manager and Coach within the FIH, offering worldwide clinics to further the cause of Umpiring.

This unlikely pair was to work as an inseparable unit right through to today. WC Eagles was not even around when one day a group of pre-College girls phoned Richard to ask if he could give them some hockey training before they arrived at University. He actually had an underground cellar below his offices which could take a number of large American vehicles, but could also double as a low roof hockey training area. Convincing his partner reluctantly at first to take on the girls, word soon spread around about Jun's natural aptitude to coach the game. This became a regular occurrence in 2005, and so popular was the training, that Jun was forced to offer a Summer Camp attended by 43 players in the prosperous outer suburbs of Philadelphia, the real capital and focal point for American field hockey.

Expansion was inevitable as Jun and Richard decided to form the WC Eagles Field Hockey Club for girls, and soon they were attending, without a real home for themselves, open, indoor and 7-a-side regional tournaments. Their home pitch was a hired school one and sometimes the facility of a local University was used for home matches. Again, there was a dilemma – they kept winning all the competitions and Americans gravitate towards winners!! Soon they were going further afield for competition, to Florida for the annual Disney event, to the National Indoor Festival and to the rapidly enlarged National Tournament for young field hockey clubs.

The pair knew early on that there was a place for hockey clubs in America, as after all they had been successfully achieved in soccer with a healthy contribution from both genders. Indeed Richard and Jun really were reflecting what was to grow incredibly fast in the next ten years, that men and women would work together to offer a new wing for hockey, an American modern club system, all be it a Junior Club one at that.

Even though Jun had experienced tremendous early successes, she still was clear on introducing her philosophy to the game which was,

"to prepare the players for College field hockey through total player development, whereby they learn the modern skills and tactics of the game under pressure of time and space in a competitive environment"

Her attention to detail in offering team training and individual lessons was constant throughout the year and augmented at her Summer Camps where International players and coaches of the quality of Jorge Lombi, John Shaw, Jamie Dwyer, Mark Knowles and Gavin Featherstone conducted long and short summer clinics for thousands of aspiring girls over these years.

With the burgeoning costs of hiring pitches and travelling across the states for festivals, Jun and Richard reached the challenging conclusion that they must go it alone and have their own home hockey facility. The Hockey Dynamic was about to click in, and how!!

By 2009, WC Eagles were already National Club Indoor Champions at U14, U16 and U19 levels and had walked away with the National Outdoor Festival Event at U16 and U19 levels. There were now just too many girls knocking on their door for club membership.

Richard moved mountains to gain the financial backing to build the biggest custom-made indoor hockey centre in the world, boasting three F.I.H. top class courts with a state of the art TigerTurf outdoor synthetic field directly in front of the club building. In typical fashion, he wanted it up and running within 16 weeks!! Impossible, as the site opposite the location of Longstreth's Super Hockey store in rural Pennsylvania, surely would normally take double that time to erect.

As usual, the dynamic duo surrounded themselves with the best of friends, associates and parents who would all contribute to complete the job. Private enterprise was the middle name of Joe Neuber, who had made his fortune in concrete on a national scale. His daughter played left defender for the WC Eagles U16 team. So, Joe just tore into the job taking charge of specifications and working with a highly reputable and charismatic building group drawn from the Amish Community. Elam King was the boss, a marvellous person that lived to the letter of the law of his faith in dress and in belief. How did the Philadelphia boy, the former Rock drummer work with a Pennsylvania Dutch steel erector with the project overseen by an Anglo-Chinese hockey combo?

The answer of course was miraculously well. WC Eagles was the hockey home of Jun and Richard's wildest dreams. It was up and running with the numbers now exceeding over 300 members as the club brought in coaches on a full-time professional basis from Argentina, Britain, Uruguay, China and Australia over the five years following completion in 2009. This international flavour permeated the club as it embarked on regular overseas tours and competitions to add to the field hockey experience of the ambitious girls.

As they say, the rest is history. By 2014, the Eagles had completed an amazing run of back to back National Championship wins at all levels, both indoor and outdoor as they enjoyed the status of being ranked the Number 1 Club in the United States. They were contributing heavily to the U.S. Junior age group teams right up to the U21 Junior World Cup and Senior Indoor National Team level as well. From 2009 to 2014, they produced a staggering 187 players for College entry to compete in the NCAA field hockey championships.

WC Eagles truly had outstripped anything that even the National Association was creating, and it was done with little fuss, but through sheer hard work. Today, dozens of indoor teams in neighbouring states and further afield travel to the club to train and use the facilities which are fully booked from 8 am. to 10 pm. on all seven days a week.

What was it like to be a small part of this new phenomenon, an American field hockey club with all the trimmings! This author made his mild contribution by appearing at virtually every Summer Camp for ten years, but was the first to recognise the community that had been built up around the growing WC Eagles Club that essentially aided Jun and Richard to achieve their success story. Maybe it is best to leave this chapter to a very willing parent from these years who witnessed it all. Indeed, the whole family played their part in acknowledging a global common theme in the story of WC Eagles. Club and Community going forward together, take note English Soccer clubs, you just can't beat it!!

These are the parent's words: -

"Clubs depend on the parents to contribute in ways that go beyond the obvious time commitment and financial support of the players. Parents that are able, volunteer at all levels to the functioning of the facility at WC, anything from tending the snack bar, emptying trash cans during tournaments, organising fund raisers, etc - whatever they feel they can do to help out. Jun and Richard expect players to give 100% at all times, no exception. Team practices are intense both physically and mentally as the WC Eagles teaching and coaching methods are not for the faint of heart. Parents are expected to be equally committed and supportive. Committed parents are one of the keys to any club's success; the level of commitment required is impressive and that includes a hefty financial commitment. On the surface it may not appear to be a sport that requires a huge output of money in order to participate, but all top clubs travel to local competitions most weekends and the top national level competitions are, in all practicality, mandatory. WC Eagles travel to at least four major events each year, none of which are held in their home state of PA. In addition, select players have travelled to Argentina, China and New Zealand to gain international playing experience. Fundraisers contribute a portion of costs, but the main expenditure comes from parents.

It may be considered that since a strong work ethic and commitment is expected of the players and parents, you tend to see a higher social economic background for many of the parents at WC. One could argue that these are highly competitive hard working parents who have been successful in work and this reflects on their children. There is an understanding of the value of what a good club has to offer; the ability for their daughters to have the best training at the best facility with plenty of competition and the recognition and clout that comes with playing for a top club. Ultimately it's the hope that scholarship money will come their way to help the ever increasing cost of college tuition. Playing for a top university program with a scholarship is an ultimate goal for many of the girls and their parents. (An attitude and goal that makes the American system of play very different from other countries).

Considering the time and financial obligations involved, some parents tend to feel resentful when their support does not include involvement with coaching methods. This is strictly Jun and Richards's program and parents' opinions do not have a place at the table.

It is helpful to understand that Jun comes from the Chinese Athletic system; a way of life most Americans cannot even begin to understand. Many top level Chinese athletes have an unrelenting appetite for hard work, complete dedication and focus. Enduring physical pain is accepted as a natural part of training. Athletes take great pride in their sport for the honor of their country and family. Jun came from a system where if you didn't perform well at practice you might not eat that night. A Chinese parent naturally expects self-reliance from their children from the get-go. American parents approach childrearing from the complete opposite end of the spectrum, Americans tend to coddle their children and protect them from hardship. Needless to say, opinions on how players are coached or treated are quite different from Jun's perspective and the parents. But it is this "hard wired" work ethic that comes from Jun and Richard that is the great contributing factor to the clubs success. Like, attracts like. The typical parent at WC would be considered successful by most standards; doctors, lawyers, business owners, financial advisors, etc. No matter what the background, many of the same attributes come to mind; driven, goal oriented, competitive, self-reliant, and a desire to improve their circumstances - qualities valued by Jun and Richard.

When Jun and Richard made the decision to build a new world class facility, parents came forward to offer their time and labor to help make the facility a reality. One parent, Joe Neuber, volunteered to be the General Contractor for the project and with his direction the allotted 9 month project was completed in only 4 and a half months - A feat that required all of the same qualities from the contractors that June and Richard expect from their players. Neuber epitomizes many or the qualities described above; a self-made concrete contractor who barely graduated from high school who through hard work and dedication went on to become one of the leaders in concrete construction in the country. His understanding the level of commitment required in order to complete a project of this scale on time and on budget led him to the logical conclusion to use like-minded subcontractors such as Elam King. Elam of Keystone Steel Structures, an Amish steel erector was also key in delivering on time and on budget. King's Amish upbringing shares the same commitment and expectation of success. The Amish are known for their strong work ethic. Amish have a strong sense of commitment to God, family, church and community. Their faith is rooted in a literal interpretation of the Bible and in the Ordnung, the rules of conduct handed down for generations, regularly reviewed and earnestly taken to heart. Amish parents train their children to participate in family chores from the time they are able to understand simple commands. If you spend any time with the Amish you will quickly realize how physically fit they are; "Hard work pays a good dividend" is a common saying among the Amish. Interestingly Jun, Neuber and King all come from very different backgrounds but they share many similar qualities, all qualities that lead to success."

The Oldest Hockey Club Tournament ;
At a Polo Club !!

Jun Kentwell leads the way: China's former international coaching America's future stars

America's biggest and best:
The Training Center, Home of WC Eagles Field Hockey Club

-Part G-
Institutes and Academies

Surely it had been a foregone conclusion. What, Australia lose to New Zealand in an Olympic final? Well, they actually achieved that fate in 1976. Not only that, but the Australian Olympic Committee was not best pleased with the overall performance of Aussie sport in Montreal. In fact, the Aussie men's hockey team had gained the highest medal, a silver one, with only four other bronze medals in twenty events. Prime Minister Fraser was beside himself in frustration!!

Australian hockey to date in world terms was a male preserve as the women would start their FIH debut seven years later. The men up until this point had always been the bridesmaid, never the bride. So, what would it take to upgrade the level of performance to winning a world tournament? To some extent this would be taken out of hockey's hands as government and state overseers were intent on devising a plan which would cover a multitude of sports.

Before any concept could be laid down on the table, it was necessary to identify where the problem areas were located that had filled the nation with doubt for the first time over their sporting prowess. It is within this remit that the subject matter is hockey, but many of the issues to be raised were very much common to the perceived failings of other Olympic disciplines as well.

Firstly, there was the geographical isolation from other competing nations. No one could shrink the miles, but there needed to be a real attempt at the top end of the sport to engage more in overseas test matches, including ones of a developmental nature, and to attract some of the key hockey nations like Holland, England and India to tour Australia and promote the game in all regional centres.

The real dilemma was actually one of internal distances, even within states. There was just too much variation between Country Districts and urban centres, between the standards set in differing states, and between state and international hockey at all levels. New developments, ideas on training, match and tournament preparation, were all often locked into states thousands of miles apart and often cautiously guarded.

In simple terms, notably with the young at base level, hockey players were exposed to differing approaches in coaching and training without a common thread running through how the game should be played. Representative players would only don their state colours at the annual Championships as there was great competitive rivalry but little fusion on shared goals and development.

The Aussies, at this stage, knew full well that Europe had fully recovered from post-war traumas and was forging ahead in the pursuit of organised leisure and sport. The club system was already well integrated in Germany, Holland and Belgium in terms of competition in men and women's national leagues, indoor and out. In addition, allocated training centres specifically for the needs of sports like hockey and football were well established at Papendaal , the Sports Schule in Cologne and at Lilleshall in England. The Asians, in turn, stuck to their monthly internal tournaments and training camps to prepare their teams for national and international competition.

As the administrators knocked their heads together, they knew Australian hockey was there or thereabouts, but they also recognised that Europe had undergone a continental transformation in the 70's as hockey was quickly learning from the highly successful Dutch and German football philosophies and applying parallel training methods. After Montreal, the Aussie sporting bodies were asking themselves whether it would continue to be good enough to assemble squads for overseas tours or tournaments just for two days at a departure point and trust that true Aussie grit and determination would do the rest.

The answer was a resounding no, and a no which would demand a more holistic approach to both hockey and sport development. That really meant government involvement if the scale of improvement and progression was to be met in the ensuing years. Hockey clubs with woeful to average facilities scattered over hundreds of square miles had to become a thing of the past. The Associations did acknowledge that this would not go down well with the community clubs serving outlying districts.

They accepted that the very best of Australian players were not necessarily rising to the top, and that talent identification had to be a new major objective for the AHA and the AWHA. How would it be possible to attract the best young talent to one spot to be professionally trained? Surely it would have meant enormous upheaval to transfer the talent pool to the urban areas. Once there, how could these young players survive without remuneration, or at the very least, some exposure to further educational opportunities?

Yes, the talent was dispersed alright, from upcountry towns in Queensland like Maryborough and Townsville, to the rural back country of Tamworth and Scone in New South Wales, onto Melbourne's big clubs and then finally five hours away by plane to Western Australia in Perth. How the Aussies envied the Dutch with their Premier clubs located just an hour apart by car!!

Even if the government and states could get the hockey hopefuls to one spot, what constituted that place in 1977? Nothing that could in any way support the type of programmes anticipated? The small clubs and schools were insufficient, but maybe, just maybe the State Universities could offer real potential in extending their facilities. In the future, they would certainly need Astroturf pitches, but they had not yet quite arrived in Australia. Facilities like that would require land which was not such a problem, but they would also incur an enormous capital investment nationwide. Astroturf playing fields, as noted earlier, were a North American phenomenon, and as a sporting innovation were definitely demanding top dollar and overseas installation expertise.

One more drawback for hockey's development was the total lack of full-time coaching. Indeed, coaching really belonged to the plentiful supply of physical educationalists in the school system who would give of their spare time to help connect the ends between school, club and state level play. Many of these men and women would then have loved to have turned "Pro", but there simply was no demand nor was there any funding to transfer these solid teachers into coaches. Two prominent men, both teachers by training, were to play a pivotal role in devising the potential new concept for hockey, and more importantly, its execution over the next two decades. They were Richard Aggiss and Frank Murray.

Even diehard Aussies knew then that the coaching experience base just was not there, but at least these physical education specialists, given new opportunities in hockey full-time, would flock to the market place, and move out of state to service the fresh expansion of the game Down Under. Yet, as shown before, at this point, they were never to possess the finely tuned coaching skills of their European counterparts, men like Horst Wein, Roger Self and Wim Von Heumann.

The Aussie hockey community needed focal points to encourage the growth and success of the sport. Yet, do not forget for one moment that there were two organisations running the game in Australia. Hockey, of course, had been passed down the line from British origins, and despite covering a wide area of hockey infiltration, the wretched hand of gender separation was planted into two Associations, the AHA and the AWHA, with differing agendas for men and women. As time moved on, this was just another obstacle to gaining wholesale government and state support. In fact, it took, can you believe, until the year 2000 and a host Olympics to bring the two wings of the game together!!

Common focal points for concentrating talent, with facilities to include tracks, gyms and synthetic pitches, necessitating full time professional staffing and libraries were envisaged to complement the sports science evolution. Now, to achieve these ends, it was only feasible if they could accommodate a range of national and Olympic sports at one National Sports Institute. The resultant investment could then be spread across Federal, State and National Governing Body funding, and where possible, to extend already existing centres for sport. The eight sports highlighted to be moved to the nation's capital of Canberra were to be swimming, athletics, basketball, football, netball, rowing, weight lifting and gymnastics in 1981.

The concept of centralised institutes was not just a reaction to poor results at the Montreal Olympics. Professor John Bloomfield was enrolled by the Australian Sports Commission in 1973 to visit a number of European countries to observe what had been the start of specialised academies. Even Barcelona Football Club whose motto of, "it's more than just a club" hosted specific sections for basketball and hockey to entice a huge membership to partake in sport as recreation in the Catalan city. His subsequent report hit the desk of Allan Coles who headed the Australian Sports Institute study group. Their task was to promote a feasibility study to discover if and how Australia, through extensive government and state aid, could resurrect and facilitate sport as a major part of the national culture. This was to be the birth of the Australian Institute of Sport in Belcomen, Canberra in 1981.

Why then, from 1975, did it take so long to implement the plan? And why was hockey missing, as a silver medal sport, from the eight selected to further their causes in Canberra? The turbulent years of international boycotts were about to begin and internally the Australian Government, the States themselves, the AHA and the AWHA and sponsors all had to share the cost burden in major building projects. Another complication was in the lead up to the 1980 Moscow Games. There was considerable disagreement within these diverse factions in whether Australia should attend or join the huge western boycott of the Games. Internal wrangling sadly cost the Institute programme several years in its implementation.

As for hockey, even though given Institute status, there was another problem; - where should it have been located? More debate followed, but finally the decision to place the Institute in Perth, "the most isolated city in the world, more than four hours by plane from anywhere."

Surely an Institute should reflect centrality to the hockey population? Perth would be costly for personnel to continually fly back and forward from the east. Frankly, the city, although expanding, could not hold a candle to Sydney or Melbourne or contain the capital assets of Canberra. Just maybe it was because Perth was marginal to all those competing interests that it seemed an interesting proposition.

There were, of course, hockey reasons beyond politics. Western Australia, for some time had produced championship winning inter-state teams that had consistently won annual tournaments with a concentration of international players like Ric Charlesworth, David Bell, Peter Haslehurst, Craig Davies and Terry Walsh. The organisation of club hockey in Perth was especially tight with a marked influence from ex-pat Indians directly leading back to past Indian touring teams.

Add to that was Perth's excellent schools system, both public and private that were well established as nurseries for team sports like hockey. They had established close ties with the vastly expanding University of Western Australia, which really meant there was already in place a thriving young hockey community. If modern facilities could be extended onto the campus of the University, it would even be possible to host centralised games for clubs at weekends which would definitely augment an Institute programme on a practical level. Equally, the University and local TAFE centres(further education colleges) were to become progressively more important to the concept for offering both full-time and part-time areas of study for prospective Institute scholars.

To place a detailed subjective handle on the Institute and the later State Academy system, we need to gain an insider's view and experience. Brent Deans, an ex- State player himself and part of a family steeped in Aussie hockey, was very much part of this process as he acted as Coaching Director for ACT (Australia Capital Territory) during these years. Not only had he overseen operations within ACT, but he was later to take the academy system out of Australia and introduce it as Performance Director for Scotland later in his career. So, in Brent's words and recollections, on his formative coaching years, the interview revealed several home truths:

GAV : In one short line, what was the aspiration of the Institute?
BD : The Institute concept, started in 1984, was the hockey system we know today, a number of athletes in one centre training full-time (20 – 30 hours per week)

GAV : When and why did the concept devolve to Perth and were there any teething problems out there?

BD : WA had the majority of the players at this time, and with the bulk of the national team coaches based there as well, the hockey in Perth was seen to be the best in the country and they had the early facilities to support the programme and significantly the dual cooperation of the University with the State Government.

There were initial issues with the local competition, but a solution was that the institute athletes went into a draft for the clubs. The clubs were able to pick players based on where they finished the previous season : e.g. The team that finished last would get first pick. While this appeared to be reasonable, the Institute athletes were not always available as they were frequently away at tournaments.

GAV : How did school and club players get to be part of the Institute, and were they residential?

BD : It was a long way from school and club athletes to receive an Institute scholarship. Firstly athletes would need to be selected in their State aged or senior team, and for AIS scholarships, the athletes were compelled to be in Perth on a residential programme. In the early days the AIS purchased a block of flats to house the athletes, latterly that evolved into individual house sharing amongst players.

The concept of State Institutes (Academies) started around '89, and the hockey non-residential centres within the States offered distinct variations depending on size and hockey populations. For instance, in Canberra, the athletes lived at home and came in to train at the hockey centre two or three evenings a week. In the bigger states athletes travelled in for weekend camps.

GAV : What prompted the move to diversify from the original Institute base at Perth to the States ?

BD : There were many reasons, but more government investment meant more scholarships and coaching positions. Running parallel to this was the demands of all the other states wanting a piece of the action, and the unwillingness of a minority of players wishing to uproot.

GAV : Was there a permanent professional full-time coaching staff, and what did the facilities include?

BD : The National Coaches were the AIS hockey coaches. The assistant coaches were the U21 National coaches with at least one full-time coach per State, the bigger ones had men and women's coaches. All states began with synthetic pitch facilities and indoor areas which were funded by the state governments.

GAV : Once selected for an Institute squad, what was the route to the National senior and junior teams?

BD : To be selected would mean that you were in either group. Scholarships would vary depending on what was happening the following year. For instance, the year of a Junior World Cup would see the JWC squad all in Perth.

GAV : Such a system with grant aid and scholarships surely demanded contracts?

BD : This was a hazy area, as the only binding aspect was a contractual agreement signed by the players, but it left incredible latitude for either scholar or coach to terminate. This situation did improve as the state and Institute programmes evolved with greater funding.

GAV : What happened to these young players' educations when they were centred at the Institute, notably their tertiary education?

BD : In the early days, athletes were just left to themselves to sort out what they did outside the programme. Some studied and some worked. As it grew the athlete education became a much bigger part of the process with most players doing units of study either at University or at further education colleges. There still were some in the National teams that were just hockey bums working part-time at whatever they could get.

GAV : Surely this Government –led concept never could replace the pride and rivalry between the old states. Where was the real internal competition?

BD : For many it was a passing of an era, but in the early Institute days, it was still very much home grown players playing for their home states as they did fly back for the Championships. The only state that did have an issue with this was WA, as the Institute emptied on such occasions. Once the state academies were operating, it was essential to compare the relevant strengths, and so began the franchised National League where players could move around, which increased the quality of the lesser states. An example would be with our Canberra Lakers where both internal imports and an external one in Bobby Crutchley from England shot us up in the national rankings. We had almost come full circle with an outcome being an increase in the quality of depth for the teams.

GAV : Sum up the positive changes that the Institutes and Academies provided over the decades?

BD : The big impact was the introduction of the State Academies which increased the pool of players and coaches. State rivalries were reborn with a much broader base at a higher level of play.

Brent's comments were forthright and to the point, but some background context has to be added to really comprehend what were the driving factors that made the Institute system actually work. The core of the matter was that it was funded from the top- down, above hockey. Even in 1976, the Australian Sports Commission had realised that the men's silver medal had been achieved despite losses at the Games to Holland, Argentina, New Zealand and a 6-1 thrashing at the hands of India. Something had to be done.

Once the AIS centre was up and running in Perth in 1984 with the women following suit in '86, the upturn in the respective performances in the immediate years was remarkable. Many Aussie hockey authorities would accurately point to the fact that these triumphs were moulded and crafted in the original state championship system of old, and that the new academies merely put the icing on the cake. Whatever, the men carried off the World Cup gold in London in '86 and the women triumphed to Olympic gold in Korea in '88. Naturally the Sports Commission wanted to reinforce these early successes more broadly by promoting hockey through the public's participation. It was a fact that the number of registered players in women's hockey doubled in the four years that followed the Seoul Olympics.

For government agencies, it was a case of the health of the nation as much as the individual success of hockey. The modern world with all of its extremes had caught up with Australia, and the Aussies had felt it the duty of government to provide the impetus, "the role model effect", and the facilities to encourage its population to take their health more seriously again. Hockey as a game for men and women, young and old, could achieve this. The old days of a dip in Bondi, playing ball on a bare patch footie field or chalking a wicket on the nearest tree may have been the outset for Don Bradman or Dawn Fraser, " but sport was a more complex matter now." Really?

Back in Perth, the initial aura of the Institute had been challenged by the end of the 80's decade. Homesickness and some issues of personal indiscipline were in evidence in these early years. Brent alluded to the fact that the educational side of the scholarships was rather left open to the individual's choice, and their choice was often part-time or no time. The scholarships themselves certainly covered basic living costs for the young athletes, but no more than that. The less qualified would have sought employment that was in no way supervised or beneficial in terms with blending in with the lifestyle expected of an international athlete.

Other players from across the country, though offered full AIS scholarships, notably the younger ones, were turning them down as they did not want to be parted from their families, friends and further education in their home states. Although the AIS was to be a permanent fixture in Perth, a kind of hockey evolution was taking place where the Sports Commission was reading the signals and acting in recommending future centralisation within states.

Scholarship levels increased under the government initiative termed "The Next Step", incorporating an investment of central finance of $217 million to all sports over what was now the tried and tested four year plan from 1989. Also note that this figure did not include state monies or the contributions that sponsors would have gifted.

At this juncture with the States issuing an unprecedented building programme on facilities, it was time for sports to be identified with selected regional centres. Diving and cricket in Brisbane, sailing in Sydney, were well positioned climatically, and developed to the extent of their infrastructural progress. All new builds had to cover areas for nutrition, sports medicine, video analysis, strength and conditioning arenas as well as sports specific requirements like floodlit AstroTurf pitches. Hockey had indeed led the way to specialisation in Perth five years earlier, and it had been a model that was bearing fruit.

In addition, "Next Step" needed to enlarge the human content to improve sporting performance where, at the top, they employed National Coaching Directors for each sport and instigated a Coaching Accreditation scheme which yielded a staggering 62,000 members for the Olympic sports alone. During this post-Seoul period and into the next four years of "Maintaining the Momentum," there was a real push to send AIS representative teams to Europe and Asia and to host visiting international squads at the new showcase State centres for Test matches. The climax of such policies was the Aussies' hosting a first for them, the Men's World Cup in Sydney in 1994.

Huge sums were placed at the other end of the scale where interactive computer programmes were introduced to attract young children to hockey and sport in order to promote further excellence and participation. The essential yardstick of success in "Next Step" and "Maintaining the Momentum" was to broaden the participation base of the triangle.

Even though the latter was to take the total of government spending to $293 million to all sports through to '96, it was soon to be overshadowed by the decision of the International Olympic Committee to award Sydney the Games of 2000. A new $135 million investment called "The Olympic Athlete Programme" was designed for the aspiring sports personnel of this "lucky generation".

It sounded just like another windfall, but this time the "bosses" meant business, as hockey with others had to have a sound sports development plan in place to cover the broader issues, as well as providing focus for their top athletes. Indeed, the Sports Commission made sure that performance targets would be directly linked to the generous levels of financial assistance. The National Training centres in the States were located to enhance individual and team achievement with all the support services the Institutes and Academies could supply. The funding was to be largely in federal hands, but the management and upkeep was the responsibility of the state academies.

The players responded magnificently with a continual stream of women's gold medals and men's bronze for the entire 90's decade. The concentration of hockey talent was the result of the combined asset of supremacy in infrastructure over competing nations, with the shrewd and methodical coaching of Ric Charlesworth and Frank Murray. Pointedly, both men had been there at the outset of the AIS back in the early 80's in Perth, and progressing forward were instrumental not only in the succeeding decade's success, but also in aligning new coaching ideas into the next century. In short, they had positioned Australia at the very front of the line when it came to tournament hockey honours.

How much of all this was attributable to Ric and his charismatic approach is very debatable. After cleaning up gold at two Olympics and the same at two World Cups prior to and including Sydney, the Aussie women have won nothing in 15 years. Same system prevails, wonderful climate, experienced coaching staff; so, where lies the difference? Did Ric Charlesworth just inherit a gifted generation of Alison Annan, Nicky Hudson, Rochelle Hawkes and others. The author would suggest we all look behind the scenes and identify one enormous change in Australian hockey that took place in 2000. The Men and the Women joined forces under one umbrella.

As one former Australian international, Sharyn Simpson explained to me, having worked in a prominent developmental role leading up to Sydney:

"We were still separate Associations then, and treated as such by the states and the government. In effect, we were working off a double budget. Whatever Ric wanted, he got with interest as he never had to compete with anyone for his slice of the cake. It was all very different after Sydney

2000 when we amalgamated on the same hockey budget that had to be shared between the two former Associations. You must have noticed over there in Europe the scarcity in AIS teams on tours coming to play Europe's best in recent years? Several years of general economic downturn could not have helped either, but within hockey I noticed there seemed to be an increasing bureaucratic interference from political bodies that simply was not apparent in the earlier days. This to my mind has placed a stranglehold, notably on the women's game, where coaching innovation has disappeared along with the standards of Ric's glory years with the Hockeyroos."

The true test on the Institute system would be whether you could readily superimpose it onto another country's hockey, and make it work in a totally different environment. England and Great Britain were drifting into neutral gear in the closing years of the century, never having built upon a successful gold medal in Seoul and a bronze in Barcelona in '92. They needed a boost, so their solution was to appoint two performance directors, one for England in the form of Chris Spice, and ironically the ACT man himself, Brent Deans for Scotland.

There were many who were more than skeptical about how Brent would face the challenge of adjustment to an under-performing nation which was cash-strapped and heavily reliant on an established base of underfunded schools, universities more known for their after-hockey activities and a very sparse club network. As for Chris Spice, he surely had inherited the proverbial pot of gold. In 1997, Sport England had announced through the kind auspices of the National Lottery a huge investment into elite Sport with a view to performing at the 2000 Games. England, and Great Britain in particular, would have plentiful resources to fund the preparation along the Aussie model of the previous decade.

Unlike his countryman north of the border, he had real potential to work with as the men's and women's U21 teams had recorded solid performances at the 1997 Junior World Cups, both finishing in record high positions, and the two senior teams in the form of Great Britain finishing 4th and 6th at the '96 Atlanta Games. Could Spice, with all these assets take the programme on to collect medals? Surely it was an attainable goal with the capital investment provided. In Dean's situation, it was more a case of producing best practice, and improving the infrastructural and development side of the game in Scotland. So, two differing motivations, both covered in the Aussie model of institutes and academies, but both had the common bond of having to deliver on the British stage. How did they fare?

Spice had relished the thought of converting another nation to what he had just experienced as a support performance coach in Australia. Along with him, the Brits had signed up the experienced Barry Dancer as Head Coach for England and Britain's men. So, with two prominent Aussies at the helm, what could possibly go wrong?

Have you ever heard of the expression of trying to fit a square peg into a round hole? Spice really thought he could just reproduce the Aussie blueprint and stamp it onto, at the time, a very compliant bunch at the top of the sport in England. Indeed, academies and institutes were becoming buzz words at all levels as even Church social groups were attracting believers to their Sunday academies. Then, another initiative was born ..... that of the play-off. At the end of a long seven month season, the winning champion league team would have to accept they were not champs after all. They would then face, over two weekends, games against those teams that had trailed in their wake, who had finished Number 2, 3 and 4 to determine the real gold medalists.

Club hockey, the very base of not just English, but European hockey as well, was being tampered with not only in this way, but also in how Spice regarded the club ethic. In Australia, it was very easy to take players from a club base, tempting them to prioritise towards a state academy and effectively take on the reins with that player's development from there on in. British hockey could claim that the club had far deeper roots than that, like in football, it represented the local community and club members who had often invested a great deal of time, energy and guidance towards these emerging players. In short, the player belonged to the local club, not to Wessex Leopards(a mythical name to represent the South-West) or England Hockey.

It all seemed a very artificial experiment with lots of make-over gloss and dollops of political correctness, but where was the substance? Certainly while the money was there and with a new group of administrative and coaching personnel to always be there to spend the resources, Spice and his cohorts enjoyed their time in the limelight. However, early poor results at the World Cup of Utrecht, 9th position with the women, and the men just hanging on to 6th were reinforced at the Sydney Olympics two years later with the women not even qualifying in the top 8 and again, the men just moving sideways.

There had been little impact also at junior levels as European results left England firmly behind the Dutch and the Germans, whilst the girls nose-dived at the U21 World Cup in 2001 in Argentina into the 9 to 12 placing.

Club performances merely followed the national team trend with huge margin losses in Euro club championships.

Then the bombshell was dropped in 2001. The English Hockey Association was bankrupt, broke and seemingly had few sympathisers as Olympic results had plummeted with scandalous reports in the newspapers of inter-squad disharmony in the women's team with the captain, Pauline Stott, admitting publicly that she had been close to a nervous breakdown during her Olympic experience. For four years, England, through the guidance of a Performance Director who had never coached as a Head Coach at Senior International level, had simply gone backwards, and had the dubious distinction in the two succeeding years to have two name changes in order to offset its financial difficulties. It would take the new England Hockey organisation the best part of a decade to unravel the mess that had been created, and many commentators would assert that hockey was really only to be saved by the appointment of London to host the 2012 Olympic Games.

The Institute system was a failure from the start in a country like England with very well established procedures and traditions which just were not in evidence in such a geographically diverse nation like Australia. It was change for change's sake with the human element more geared up for political issues rather than improving the range and performance of the game.

In Scotland, did Brent Deans have to face similar challenges?
His role as performance director, and playing a significant role in executive matters over an extended period of twelve years was to make Scottish hockey as efficient as could be achieved. There had to be a sense of realism here, and might I suggest that Brent had ideal experience here from Australia in being previously involved with ACT (Australia Capital Territory) in Canberra. This was a small state in relation to the whole, and little was expected from it in terms of scale and performance.

The same could be said of Scottish hockey in relation to Great Britain. Brent soon acknowledged that expecting Scotland to compete at World level was unrealistic, but European and Commonwealth objectives were feasible. During his tenure, the Scots men have mainly kept a placing in the Euro B Division whilst the women have boomeranged between A and B. So they have not set the world on fire, but remain indoors and out a competitive European nation, which considering their meagre population, has been some achievement.

Getting more players out there, notably the young talent , has been a frontline policy for, as in Australia, there was a wider campaign for improving the nation's health through sport. The fact that Brent Dean's years saw greater participation, which was supported by a professional full-time staff of 23 men and women reflects his sense of realism and more evidence of the increased professionalism that he brought to the sport in Scotland.

As in Aussie, there were many channels for funding, through UK Sport, Sport Scotland and the Great Britain Olympic Group to enhance a variety of programmes in Scotland. Yes, Scottish hockey had to be well audited and provide good governance reviews with positive financial balance sheets. This they achieved with regular consistency and in 2010, following an intensive review, Scottish Hockey was awarded the most proficiently run sport in Scotland. Indeed, during a period in the century's first decade, the Scottish Hockey's financial reserves met healthy levels, quadrupling at this time.

It would be trite to suggest that this was attributable to the influence of a Performance Director, but there was no doubt, notably in the years leading up to the London Games in 2012, that Brent had travelled that route before and was very familiar with handling the ways of big government in its interaction with national governing bodies. This was the result of Britain taking on many of the lessons that the Australians had learned from the Sydney Olympic experience. Sport now took on not only more specialists around the field of play, but also there emerged a whole pack of professional marketeers, sponsors, lawyers and accountants for the whole to be an efficient working entity. Brent had recognised that fact in the early days of "Institutes and Academies" back in Canberra, when he did compete with far more powerful states for a piece of the Aussie cake.

Surprisingly, the Academy System of Australia with its equivalent regional centres for hockey, its improved synthetic facilities and the installation of a very well defined administrative sector worked to further the game in Scotland in Brent Dean's time there more so than in any other era. In England's case, it was entirely different, as on the pitch aspirations were the priority. Whereas Institutes and Academies brought the diverse nature of the Aussie states together harmonising their play, and professionalising their many hockey enthusiasts, these assets were already there in the clubs of England. Chris Spice did not seem to appreciate this, and therefore ran into serious crossfire with club administrators, and furthermore approached the playing side of the game in a very didactic manner, stressing the way to play was the Aussie way.

There is no doubt that specialised centres for hockey training, development and performance were elements which have contributed to all sports expansion, and when they are mutually spread across large distances that exist in places like Australia, Canada, South Africa and the USA, they rapidly dispel regional contrasts and formulate a common national playing style which has typified the Aussie approach since the inception of the Academies twenty five years ago. This has brought with it a consistency of standards to national and international play with a nation like Australia seldom ranked out of the top four in men's and women's world hockey.

However, what had not linked the system in Australia to England and Scotland was coaches and coaching philosophy with the traditions of internal competitions. These were varied and sometimes at odds with each other. The one central common denominator as the academies were transferred across the world was money, financial input. Millions were suddenly made available in Australia and England, and substantial increases occurred in Scotland through big government intervention. Were the Academies and Institutes the panacea for hockey success? We can only answer maybe, and only in the right environments. The proof of this assertion is right back where we started in Australia. Since Sydney and the 2000 Olympics, the Australian women have won no gold medals in seven attempts at World Cups and Olympics in over fifteen years.

What had happened to them? When the funding gradually dissipated during those years, performance levels went down. Not so with the men, as you could never ignore the human element. They had inherited a human fortune by the name of Charlie, Ric Charlesworth.

Australia's Specialised hockey centres, The State Academy at Canberra
(kind permission of The Australian Sports Commission)

The WAHA in Perth, home to the Australian Institute

Logging, Foam and Moonboots

The preponderance of penalty corner success around the 70's hockey world had made household names out of Kruize, Litjens, Barber, Boekhorst and Anders. Who could stop them scoring? Certainly not the Rules Board that allowed the use of the glove to control the ball and permitted hit shots inside the circle, right up until the latter part of that decade at any height of the goal.

Only nutters would stand on the line to help out their besieged goalkeepers. This author was one such nutter until a mere car accident at 50 miles per hour, something far less dangerous, enabled him to survive to observe the Bombay World Cup of 1981-2. His former team mate, Paul Barber was wheeled up to take his tenth corner of the game against the Soviet Union, but incredibly Paul could not get the ball past the amazing Vladimir Pleshakov in goal.

With a pre-determined 6 stride approach, Pleshakov then dropped like a sack of spuds to an extended horizontal barrier taking up three yards in width in front of the goal. Barber smashed it hard and harder, but the keeper absorbed it with all parts of his body for the adjacent line man to mop up the rebound to clear. Surely with just a face mask and what looked like a padded sweater/sweatshirt, everyone's only question was, "what was he wearing under the sweater?" as he always sprung up after impact. The Russians, then part of the Soviet Union, gave few secrets away in or out of hockey, but anyone who was there that day in Bombay will remember the new goalkeeping technique that thwarted the English in only a 1-1 draw.

A young English coach starry-eyed in the stands amongst good company just blurted out, "Did you see Pleshakov, he just dropped like a log in lumberjack land?" Hence, the term "logging" was born, but like all babies, it took time to develop. For sure, most commentators dismissed the Russian as half-mad, and it was a fact that the other World Cup keepers were not prepared to adopt this desperate horizontal posture.

The leading goalkeeper in the world, Ian Taylor of England fame, took particular pride in pitting his lightning reflexes against these clubbers from thirteen yards distance. At this stage, he felt there was no need to change as his record of saves at the penalty corner gave hope to all custodians at all levels. Taylor was a confident, inwardly cocky individual who relished the challenge of keeping goal in hockey after trialing with several of the country's professional football clubs. His relatively modest background had contrasted like chalk and cheese to a one-off ice hockey goaltender from Thousand Oaks, California named Bob Stiles. Little did they know then that before too long, the two of them would have at least half the answers to defending penalty corners.

Stiles was a 26 year old going nowhere in a dead end job, but had found his passion in martial arts and goaltending for his local club at Burbank Ice Rink in the Valley, north of Los Angeles. During the summer of 83 he had met one of the members of the U.S. field hockey squad whose centralised training base was at local Moorpark. Kenny Barrett had mentioned to that same English Coach that Bob had wanted to give it a go as a goaltender after watching an open video evening held the previous week.

The karate black belt arrived at the training ground where there were no goals, no lined fields, no locker rooms nor showers, just two baseball cages separated by 35 yards by 25 of natural grass. He could not believe it, that this was the Olympic focal point of the richest country in the world. Taking off his work clothes, he then pulled out of his bag an all in one white shoulder-arm-body protector. He looked, after two minutes of strapping and lacing, as if he was about to audition for Star Wars down the road in Hollywood.

The coach was literally gob-smacked when Stiles next pulled out his helmet with a frontage in the shape of a Golden Eagle's head covered in America's Stars and Stripes. Was he fit? Yes, fit for purpose? Yes, fit for the Olympic team, and that was just a matter of time. He then started his San Fernando Valley aerobics studio warm-up which was just sensational with flailing karate kicks and chops that put Bruce Lee to shame!!

"Ready to drop at Corners, eh, Bob?", inquired the coach,
"Just try and stop me", was the immediate reply as Bob fielded more than thirty screamers in succession with unflinching confidence. The coach had discovered not just a fearless goalkeeper, but a larger than life character that he had to select for the forthcoming tour of Europe and Asia that autumn. Of course he had no experience, but this guy who was not the most educated or worldly of individuals, wanted to match his skills with the integrated Cooper Ice Hockey gear against the Chinese and the Soviets. He was genuinely crestfallen when he was informed he was only to play against Pakistan, Spain, France and Great Britain!!

Back to Ian Taylor that December in 83, he didn't have much to do against, what he thought were some minnows called the USA, but the score was still 0-0 with only 6 minutes left to play at Bisham Abbey, the then home of English hockey. What he did notice was the American eagle at the other end was saving everything thrown at him, notably from Barber at penalty corners. Then a lucky break as the hit shot deflected off the out-runner's stick and flew into the top corner above the logging Stiles.

Great Britain had escaped by the skin of their teeth. They had been struggling to qualify after a poor outing at a pre-Olympic tournament in Asia which meant they were only selected as first reserve for the 1984 Olympics. Just three months later in Olympic year, and with the Russian army refusing to leave Afghanistan, Britain took the place of the Soviet Union in Los Angeles.

The British manager, Roger Self, after that defining game with the Americans at Bisham, had been consulting Taylor about the goalkeeping technique at defending Corners. Ian had admitted that after the game he had talked with Bob Stiles, but stressed to Self that he would never drop at a Corner unless he had the same type of protective gear that Stiles had been wearing for nigh on a year. There was a bit of an impasse between manager and keeper at this stage, but they knew the channels were open through Ian's former team mate- turned American coach, that Stiles could bring along his gear later in June for Taylor to test at a further game between the two nations.

The vital call was made, and Stiles' amended ice hockey contraption was now firmly in British hands. Taylor at 6 feet and one inch had already proved himself as the best vertical goalie in the world, now he was to go even further on the horizontal stage. Confident, he took on the power of Ties Kruize at a Penalty-Stroke to make a truly amazing horizontal cat-like save to send "first reserve" Britain into the semi-finals of the Olympics. After the disappointment of losing to West Germany in that semi, it was Australia with Rick Charlesworth, Terry Walsh and the fearsome Craig Davies at penalty corners for the coveted bronze medal. The Aussies fired 23, yes, 23 corners that day at Taylor's new protective gear. It was just one of the greatest goalkeeping performances of all time, as Sean Kerly equally responded with a hat-trick for Great Britain to win 3-2.

Taylor later admitted the vital role his new equipment had played, but perhaps what Ian did not appreciate at the time was a rather unusual correlation in that the technique which Pleshakov had initiated as a core defensive skill preceded the accompanying technology, the all in one Stiles adapted Cooper Upper Bodyguard, or did it? Pleshakov never yet has told his side of the story!!

It was to be all about logging from there on in for some time. Yet, another Englishman just did not see it that way at all. As a foraging striker, he never felt any sympathies for goalkeepers. He also knew that in every game, he would get clobbered by the new breed of man to man marking: central gorillas, pardon, centre defenders. His tiny shin pads were like a string vest against a shark attack. He knew, as a certain Al Capone would have us believe, it was all about protection.

So, who was this Nick Barton? Just a guy educated at Leeds and Oxford Universities as a Chemist. His mastery of chemistry was clear as he liked mucking about in the laboratories, but just how could he link that with his other life passion, that of the sport of hockey? Oh yes, he did that all right, as his work literally was to touch every goalkeeper in the world at every level for a long time to come.

Mentioned earlier, Stiles and Taylor had pioneered half the answer to defending as a modern keeper, but it was Nick Barton who not only completed the other half, but, also in turn, revolutionised protection and the changing techniques of a goalkeeper through really a very rudimentary technology.

It was not to start with goalkeeping gear. It was shin pads that drew Nick's attention. He was acquainted with future Olympian John Shaw at the time who worked for the enigmatic David Vinson who had shocked the hockey world in the early 80's by tripling the cost of his DFV hockey sticks to a minimum of US $100. The 80's decade was to be the period of equipment dynamism as Vinson along with some associates in the then West Germany began to experiment with resins to stiffen the hockey stick, forming a kind of coating around the outer fringe of the original stick.

Dave Vinson worked out of an old workshop in unfashionable Kings Lynn in Norfolk employing a bevy of young England hopefuls to act as stick factory workers. Their aim was to produce sticks which could move the ball faster, and higher in aerial play whilst outlasting the orthodox hockey stick. David's dummies in the late 70's were members of the England squad who would loan their Karachi Kings or Maharajas to Vinson to "wrap" to be returned for improved performance.

So this was the kind of culture that was controlling hockey at the time with the movement to carbon fibre sticks, kookaburra dimple balls that looked like large golf balls, and what seemed a minor modification inside the shin pad. John Shaw had shown Nick Barton the DFV pad which had revealed a thin layer of attached foam strip shaped to the contour of the shin bone. Much more comfortable to wear, Nick invested in a pair. Some months later he attended a Sports Exhibition in Olympia in West London to notice the martial arts exponents wore footwear encased with the same foam layer to protect intricate foot bones from fracture.

Like all positive innovators, he studied the composition of the foam, and was able to source a small company called Zotefoams in Croydon, South London. He journeyed across town to purchase a significant amount in order to conduct his experiments in the Bradfield College Chemistry Centre. He knew that goalkeepers were perennially complaining about bruised feet where balls had penetrated the old box or leather kickers. Nick, from the outset, suspected that foam in its original composition form might not prevent such niggly failings in the conventional kickers, but if he could expose the material to differing levels of heat, surely the pressure would alter the molecular structure of the foam.

When exposed to a certain temperature, the foam absorbed and expanded to produce a high density which, in turn contained superb qualities of protection. It was the defining moment for goalkeeping, there in the school Chemistry Lab!! Now, how would Nick present this in physical and saleable form?

He decided to produce a one dimensional product, a wrap around the foot with attached tongue and straps. Typically as an inexperienced businessman, he made a demonstration product with drawings, and basically invested in his idea by asking the Croydon Company to produce to order. They were not willing to play ball. Nick needed considerable financial investment to get his product off the ground, and to his relief, he was approached by local businessman Bill Cullis, who made a significant contribution to production costs. At around this time in the mid 80's, any innovator had to move fast, establish a patent, and gain the approval of a modern day competitor to attract the marketplace.

Here Nick was fortunate to have been at Leeds with England's Norman Hughes who was already forging ahead at Slazenger as a precursor to a professional life in sports equipment provision. Nick contacted his former captain, showed him the product and offered to Slazenger to purchase 600 pairs a year for the next ten years at 100 pounds per pair!! This was then an outrageous sum of money as Slazenger would have to put their mark-up on the item. Ian Taylor, yet again, was consulted and indeed was very keen to wear what Nick was later to christen "Moonboots for Goalkeepers". For comfort and mobility, Ian suggested some modifications in the strapping and grooves and just needed the nod to wear them at the London World Cup in 1986.

Slazenger were not prepared to take the risk of such a long term investment when notably technology was moving at such a pace, and after all, the product needed to be showcased at a major event. The Company was already heavily involved with sponsorship of the players at the World Cup, but maybe down the road, if Taylor could have a good World Cup, it would be easier to attack the market at a later stage.

They did not account for the business acumen of Bill Cullis and his hockey Company, Monarch. They took on the Moonboot, and initially marketed the kicker exclusively. It was interesting to note that in this two year period before the Olympic gold medal, it was quite common to see British club and school goalkeepers actually using the combination of Moonboots with cane leg guards!!

This factor brings us to the point of what came first, the technology or the technical advancement of the goalie's skills. During this period, below Ian Taylor were two keepers vying for that Number 2 spot in the British team, John Hurst of England and Veryan Pappin of Scotland. Both were very able keepers, and both possessed one thing in common. They pursued the idea that rather than absorb the ball and sweep clear with the stick (essentially two skills) they promoted the technique of Save-Clear. Their emphasis was to return the pace on the ball, therefore adding more power to the clearance. This brought together the era of the one touch goalkeeper actively seeking the "Ping" response as it actively cut out the close- in rebound chance that up until then all centre strikers thrived upon. Now Nick Barton claims that he always knew that the constituent properties of high density foam would produce the desired effect of returning the pace on a hockey ball. He would say that, wouldn't he!! It was all part of the technological battle to offset innovative goalkeeping equipment to counterbalance the forces that were aimed at the long suffering goalkeepers.

In just a period of five years, new faster dimple balls were unleashed from stiffened carbon fibre heavier hockey sticks on supremely truer and faster synthetic surfaces. For the first time, and it was a sign of things to come, the FIH Equipment Committee was to be kept very busy by the hockey dynamic of turf, stick, ball and goalkeeping developments. Their job was

124

to balance all forces, if you like, to keep an even keel, and did they have pressures, from subjective national coaches, the ambitions of the business world, the rules board, and even to national industries of sport equipment manufacture.

In the end, the priority was to give the goalkeepers at all levels, down to young children playing, the total protection needed in an impact game like hockey. So, in real terms, Monarch through Nick Barton finished off the job by 1988, applying for a patent in designing the complete package of high density foam leg guards to accompany the Moonboot. It looked the part now as the Goalkeeper's total surface area of protection had increased despite producing a light, mobile and most of all, popular addition to the goalie's wardrobe.

As the nineties approached, sales took off at an alarming rate for the indoor game as well, with Monarch really controlling the arena to sell on to all the main players in the market. In England, Mercian and Slazenger caught on to foam, as did TK in Germany and Brabo in Holland. It became a multi- million dollar industry worldwide, but sooner or later, like all technologies, Monarch's innovation would have to be challenged, but not quite yet. These years towards the end of the century were to be Monarch's time in the sun!!

At this stage, it is worth reviewing the impact that Ian Taylor had made in his career as a goalkeeper. These papers have minimized the role that individual personalities had made on changing the game, rather to concentrate on the dynamics of off the field influences. Taylor, as a keeper, looked and played differently to any of his predecessors. He was big but supremely athletic. His flexibility and sheer bloody-mindedness not to be beaten were often separate qualities in other goalkeepers, but with him, it was all rolled into one awesome package. Some might say he was fortunate to have been around when Nick's foam revolution was occurring, but remember Ian was all part of the finished design.

For young boys and girls, he was Moonboot Man, the coolest dude on the field. In more orthodox parlance, the FIH Committees thought so too when they awarded him the Number 1 goalkeeper in the world throughout the 80's until his retirement with the Olympic gold medal in 1988. Kids in British hockey schools and clubs were queuing up to play in goal!! To my mind, only a handful of individuals have had such a broad effect on the sport. They might include Ric Charlesworth, Shabaz Ahmad, Teun de Nooijer and Luciana Aymar. Yet, Ian's legacy was not just in how he played and the medals he won, but in defining the protection and technique that all goalies would present in their equipment.

125

Post Taylor, many of the game's changing rule base involved amendments around the circle (see Part I) and the penalty corner as the sport's administrator's grappled to retain balance. Now there were new dynamics at large in the coaching of goalkeepers as many of Taylor's first generation of "Astro –Goalies" were now offering their services as specialist goalkeeping coaches. The indoor game also was at last making inroads into how goalkeepers should include specific techniques from what was essentially a European pastime at this stage. Yet, it was a very popular game for umpires and goalies as they were central to the action in such a small surface area.

Goalkeeper preparation, training, clinics and exposure to both indoor and out made all goalies very busy for the best part of ten months of the calendar year, and in all countries as competitive hockey expanded greatly in national and international form. Indeed, as displayed in Part D, TV was playing a greater part in exposing goalkeepers in their trademark moonboots, and there were even specialist videos devoted to spreading the new techniques on a world scale. Goaltending was fashionable!! As with any technological advance, here in closed-cell production of foam for its protective result, innovation was achieved as the primary factor towards the growth of a new product. With the laboratory work complete, there then kicks in the secondary drive of investment into the finished article, and this investment is not confined to just financial input but time, energy and manpower as well. Workshop and factory sites must be sourced with a willing labour supply, whether that be local or in a different country all together.

There was no doubt that these early pioneers of foam had passed the tests of innovation and investment, and maybe they felt that they were on uncharted ground and therefore reluctant to deliver the third part of the holy trinity, that of ongoing research and development of the product. Monarch was at the helm, with Slazenger, Mercian and TK in Germany sharing the market for some time with excellent profits as part of a broad based company structure. In short, goalkeeping was only a small part of their total range of hockey equipment, and this applied equally to companies like Just Hockey in Australia and Cranbarry in the United States. It seemed like all of them had underestimated one base factor over these years in the early 90's, and that was one of cost. Where once an individual could save up to buy his or her set of leg guards and kickers, helmet and stick and it would set them back around 100 British pounds, now it was a question of high hundreds.

Many families were tested financially with such alarming cost rises as their kids desperately needed the modern gear for health and safety reasons. Even schools had to pass around pieces of a set between their squad of goalkeepers. The trend had started with David Vinson (DFV) back with hockey sticks as the thinking seemed to be that if a new technology had been introduced to the manufacturing process, that alone merited a five- fold increase in cost to the poor suffering player, many of whom were young boys and girls. This happened with sticks, with footwear, and perhaps most markedly with goalies who actually displayed on their person no less than nine separate items of protection. I know for a fact that during this period advanced drawings had been finalised for a one cover suit to be termed "The Michelin Man" in order to reduce the overall costing for schools, clubs and parents!!

Some people asked that simple question, "Why hasn't hockey taken off in the same way as football? And why have so many females worldwide turned their team allegiances to soccer from hockey?"
There you have the answer. When a hockey stick costs $ US 300, and goalkeeping gear is well over $US 1000, you can forget about kids joining the sport from ordinary backgrounds, and surely all areas of our game should be espousing the slogan "Hockey for All". The answer was that suppliers were providing infinitely better quality, and that the game as a whole was reflecting advanced technologies that went into equipment, synthetic turf, video and medical advances.

For me, I would only accept that line of argument if the product lasted the test of time with durability. Maybe old fashioned, as this certain now middle-aged coach introduced a personalised coaching board during this time which contained unique coaching aids for hockey. The designer was concerned at the suggested cost of $100 for a durable solid casing, as he went to visit a Great Britain Olympic gold medalist. "It's far too good a product, could you not have made it from cheaper materials and sold it for half the cost", he said, and added that people just throw away items, and buy another one after a year.

The trouble with the Goalkeeper gear was that it would amount to another four figure sum. Yet, the most alarming fact in this transition to high density foam was in this durability sector. Simply put, had there been enough research into how it would react to sliding across hard flooring, wet surfaces and most of all, the omnipresent sand surfaces of this era? I regret to answer that in the negative. I sincerely doubt any of them had the resources to place significant funding into research and development, because of their own cost restraints.

To their cost, somebody else did!! And this somebody else completed the story of the hockey dynamic when applied to the art and here, more pertinent, the science of goalkeeping. This refreshing innovator was to provide the missing link in the process by specialising as a Goalkeeping company, and focussing again in the vital area of research and development. Within ten years Simon Barnett and OBO would leave all the big hitters of Europe trailing in his wake as OBO would capture up to 80% of the market share of all goalkeeping gear.

After a great deal of commonsense consultations on an international footing, Simon set up his new concern in Manawatu!! Mana where? You might ask. He was based on the north island of New Zealand around Palmerston North, a hot bed of provincial hockey had been based there for some time. He himself was never a player, but a marketing man with close links to the nearby Massey University. This was to be very significant in the lift-off period for the Company as it needed research grant awards to undertake a thorough examination of the protective sports gear associated in its early days for hockey.

What they recognised was a very fragmented status quo amongst the hockey companies that failed to provide a coherent approach to servicing the needs of goalkeepers worldwide, and it was the world market that Simon Barnett was motivated towards. Increased investment came not only from 'Innovators Manawatu', but also from the New Zealand Trade and Enterprise Group that was solidly behind supporting the growth of a diverse make-up of small businesses in the country.

OBO had done its sums, and came to the conclusion that the sales price of equipment was indeed too high given the shelf life that a wide selection of keepers were continually complaining about in relation to the longevity of their kit. The New Zealand Company soon got to work on how they could take the foam product on to the next level in terms of thickness, durability and shape without incurring extra costs on the customer. A new Research and Development department scientifically took the foam apart to take it to a new dimension, and moulded a fitted shape to the size of boot for the goalie. Their research was about protection in all parts of the body with guaranteed performance. This they achieved with a close interaction with their goalkeeper clients, claiming in their marketing literature that goalies were very special people and that OBO, as a company, was formed to look after them as individuals.

The strategy worked as more and more of the world's top keepers signed up to display the OBO label at Olympics and World Cup events. Their feedback on line was a feature of their care for the players. In other words, they listened carefully to the players, the good and the bad points were all taken into consideration for modifications and future design. By 2011, OBO had won credits for their design and marketing at national level, and their workforce had now expanded to dozens in Manawatu and 42 agents all over the world.

They say, what goes round, comes round. One of Bob Stiles' rivals for an Olympic place in 1984 was Jon O'Haire who went on to play for the USA men's team for the next succeeding ten years. Jon has been a great student of all things goalkeeping over the years, a true enthusiast on the game, who in recent years has followed the technology trail to New Zealand, settling there with his family. He now takes up the story.

"I first became aware of OBO in 1995. I was still playing for the US and as such was sponsored by TK, having used Slazenger since the first moon boots arrived in '88 as well as trying the Monarch gear. The issue with all the early foam was how quickly it broke down. If you played on a regular basis, you were going through kickers every three months.

In '96, I retired and started coaching keepers. I asked OBO for a set explaining I was a coach at National level, and wanted to try them. They duly sent me a set of what were then the Proform leg guards and Robo kickers and hand protectors. They were like nothing out there, first because of the shape, but next because of the performance of the foam. Most of the existing HD kickers and pads were of naked foam which wore down from contact with the turf and compression from repeated shots. The OBO foam was bonded on the bottom of the kickers which eliminated a great deal of the abrasion wear, and the foam generally seemed to be a whole lot denser which still provided the ideal rebound and didn't break down as quickly.

They had cut the mould by providing a durable quality product at an affordable price. Later I caught up with Simon Barnett at the World Cup in '98, where he was looking to the future to present an online presence and asked me if I was interested in taking on the role as their online expert, writing tips and answering questions. I have performed this task on and off for the time since with Simon inviting me to view the operation in New Zealand in 2002. One was immediately struck with the goalkeeper culture which is central to the testing, research and design in perfecting products. OBO was very aware that little was being done by rival companies to establish their equipment as a brand, notably a goalkeeping brand. There did not seem to be as much attention to detail, whereas OBO tested extensively and took feedback very seriously. As mentioned earlier the foam was taking a beating from certain surfaces. The philosophy seemed to be, "They wear out, buy more, never a thought to change". OBO developed the bonding strip and little things like the material kicker straps were made from vinyl covered nylon cloth rather than the web nylon straps of old.

The Company continues to listen to leading keepers drawing tips from around the world. It is almost like OBO has formed a goalkeepers club around the globe with the overt appeal of its Acid colour combinations to hosting advanced goalie seminars and clinics to the Company's loyal followers. I, for one, can be included as one!!"

The OBO story is a modern one in as much as it shows how dynamic individuals, such as Simon Barnett in a far off location, have used their marketing skills to take on the hockey world and win hands down. He took the trinity of innovation, investment and development to its ultimate extent by placing all three facets under one integrated roof. That was one of his greatest achievements to secure the market, and once secured, to have developed a framework of able and trusted believers as agents worldwide.

From the chemistry lab deep down in the Berkshire Hills via the trials and tribulations of top international exponents to the research centre in Manawatu, the hockey goalkeeper has never been forgotten. Our sport has been far too dynamic to let that ever happen!!

England goalkeeper Ian Taylor; No protection, but still the best of all time

Today's walking wardrobe!!

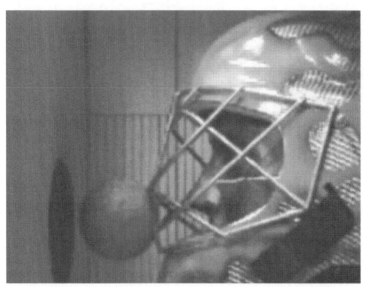

Modern high tech at OBO meets the needs of the goalkeeper specialist

OBO's Headquarters in Manawatu; a marketing worldwide success

Play by the Rules

Play by the rules, or should we say ruled by the play? How many sports in the short span of 40 years can say they have changed the ball, the pitch markings, the composition of the pitch itself and indeed a whole host of rule amendments? Those included offside, free hits, aerial ball, penalty corners, substitutions, and even the number of officials saddled with the task of delivering the laws and fair play.

The hockey umpire has often been given the tag of a dull, orthodox practitioner, the sound but unflappable policeman of a game that has been and is potentially murderous, yet because of the sensible participants, seldom have these levels of danger threatened the well being of the sport. Equally, the behaviour of the players can only be described as impeccable compared to the ranting and raving of the football variety, and to the wanton violence of the rugby codes which seldom had permeated the sport of hockey.

Maybe that was then, with the then referring to the period before 1972. Today's umpires, despite many attempts by the Rules Authorities to issue control, have faced deteriorating standards of player behaviour allied to a game which could be claimed to be the fastest team sport played with deadly stick weapons and the hardest of hard projectiles, the hockey ball.

Thus, our steady Eddie of an umpire has been subjected to a level of change by the rules umbrella and a widely changing world's idea of what is, and what is not acceptable on the sports field. Add this to the ever encroaching tentacles of related sports and their officiating trends and tendencies influencing the 'niceness' and flexibility of hockey's administrators, and you then have in the context of this work, the most dynamic adjustment that the game of hockey has had to face.

Like many of the previous topics, the Rules and the application of such by Umpires have broadly moved over the four decades from conservatism to liberalisation and have reflected two or three definitive periods which fundamentally changed the game in a radical way. This section seeks to show who were the movers and shakers and how they sculpted the modern game as we know it today.

First of all, we must examine the state of the game as umpired in 1972, and comprehend the phases of "Game Change".

GAME CHANGE

1/ The Rules Board, the Status Quo and Conservatism

2/ 1994-98, Listening to the Practitioners

3/ Technology and Experimentation

Part One – The Rules Board, the Status Quo and Conservatism

Up until 1972, there were few changes in hockey. Even the hockey stick had only amended the size of its hook in the late 60's to produce the Karachi King and its inevitable followers. There was still a ridiculous half-way line offside rule and in schools and junior hockey, the "sticks" rule of keeping the swing below the shoulder was rigorously applied with the roll-in and the use of the hand and glove prevalent at set plays. Any player dared not turn his body in any shape or form on receiving the ball as he would have committed the immortal sin of obstructing his opponent. Wherever a player ventured on the field, he was met with a multitude of rules, regulations and restrictions administered by officials born before World War 2 who respected the letter of the law, full stop.

This latter point is imperative in understanding the barriers that beset the hockey dynamic when applied to Umpiring in the latter part of the 20th century.   Rules were one thing, how they were applied in the battleground of what really mattered across the world, the actual hockey match was paramount to enjoyment and success.

Down at the local third team game on grass in 1971, no one even knew or cared about who made up or comprised these unseen and never heard of committees that determined all these restrictions. The players' motto was:

"Our's is not to reason why? Our's is but to do or die".

It was always a situation of "them upstairs" who one never questioned. Indeed many of the umpires around the world in this era were ex-players, teachers, servicemen and women, and often mates of the players. The regular Umpires rarely had contact, let alone the players, with the untouchables.

Who were these untouchables? Much was exemplified in chapter two of these papers, chronicling the close ties of the Old Boys Network in how the game developed particularly within the British Commonwealth of nations. Moreover, it was also discovered that the sport was fragmented in its administration between two sectors, the F.I.H. and the I.F.H.W.A., essentially a split between the men and women, and independently between the British commonwealth's influence on hockey with the rest of the world.

Having made that clear, this was not entirely accurate. A third powerful body exuded a hugely powerful effect over the running of the game. It was The Rules Board. This group of international committee men (in the main) would continue their reign of dominance over the sport's rules and guidelines right through until the end of the 20th century and beyond. British dominated, largely containing men over the age of 55, it was essentially the formative core that issued forth its findings to the game's dual administrators, the F.I.H. and the I.F.H.W.A.

Gradually the Rules Board's power was eroded as these two institutions merged into one in 1982, but noticeably through the ensuing amateur code decade, the Rules Board still held sway in determining any major variations in the rules and their interpretation.

By nature, the Rules Board was conservative and this cut across all its international constituents. There was a cosy inter-political game going on as they protected their own interests and cemented their position at the top of the hockey table. They were also very slow to move during this period and would often only receive advice from fellow board members or Umpires they could trust. Throughout this period in office they would seldom countenance taking advice from coaches, players, innovators, or from the commercial or publicity side of the sport.

Even though the game was crying out for leadership and action on the rules governing the penalty corner, offside and obstruction, very little was offered during the years from 1972-1994. Endless experiments ping-ponging between the North and Southern hemispheres looked at these vital areas of the game without the conviction of the Board and certainly without sufficient consultation with the players, coaches and teachers on the ground.

The Rules Board had many people's sympathies. Their duty was to set new rules and amendments that would and could be applied to hockey in all regions of the world and at all levels to men and women alike. Remember that it was only 1982 that the Men's and Women's Ruling Bodies had eventually amalgamated! The net result was often stalemate or a frustrating compromise. There was no better example of this on how the problems of offside and obstruction were reviewed over the twenty year period.

Clearly, the original space constrictions with the half-way line acting as the offside border was soon eliminated during this period, but only to be gradually eased to the 25 yard line. Years passed by as the Board tinkered with the number of defenders that could allow a player to be onside or offside. Yes, their idea all along was to open up the game to forward space, but a decade went by as the organised Europeans at all levels learned from their football counterparts how to spring the offside trap with cunning sweeper backs and disciplined back marking players.

Where did this leave the advocates of open attacking play? With the obstruction law firmly applied, a front player would try to lose his marker by forward runs only to be adjudged to be in an offside position, but could not track back to receive passes with a determined back marking defender claiming a call for obstruction to the umpire. What the rules board could not see was that for years the offside law and the interpretation of obstruction were intrinsically linked.

Certain coaches, notably those with a cross sport background, were crying out for a relaxation on the interpretation of obstruction, and a commitment to go all the way on offsides. Why not abandon both? What was stopping the Rules Board? Umpires, in the last two decades of the Millennium, were heavily weighed down by the twin tasks of blowing partial obstructions in midfield as well as having to track the highest player on the field for offside. In particular it was the Dutch and the Australians that wanted more freedom in these areas, but it was fair to say that Umpires themselves definitely were keen to get away from so many grey areas on the obstruction law.

As for the Asian world, they had always thought that the Rules Board was in the pockets of the European and Australasian powerhouses. They even went as far as to state that the Board would be reluctant to open up the game to give the more stick-skilful Indians and Pakistani the upper hand in international competition. It was a fact that offside traps and obstructions slowed the game down with the inevitable resultant set play that favoured the systematic Europeans. So, a marvellous clash of cultures was fought out between the three continental giants with the Rules Board stuck like "piggy in the middle" between Europe, Australia and Asia.

Penalty Corners were another bone of contention between the continents as the faster Astroturf surfaces were fronting up against the new Goalkeeper technologies of Part H's "Logging, Foam, and Moonboots". The Rules Board with the honest aspiration to present rules which would bring more opportunities of goals, was then faced with goalkeeper technology in the form of bigger gloves, longer sticks and excellent upper body and helmet protection.

Not only this, but that dastardly bunch, the coaches, were inventing new ways for goalkeepers to present themselves as horizontal barriers in dropping at the penalty corner defence. A balance had to be struck between the desirability to score more goals, whilst at the same time allowing the defence a fair chance at the penalty corner. Thus, the Rules Board was extremely busy over these two decades to provide balance between the ever increasing demands of the spectator and the momentum to encourage more goals in the game, with the threat of potential danger to players at all levels.

The unfortunate result of all this leading up to the World Cup of 1994 was an ongoing hesitation with these fundamental laws of the sport. The rules Board and the F.I.H. at this stage had not recognised and seemed to be blissfully unaware of the impact that synthetic turf surfaces and video technology had made on influencing hockey at their early stage. They had missed a trick here, and seemed almost antagonistic towards those innovators and technicians at ground level that were pushing to improve hockey's standing and image in showcase events such as the Olympics and the World Cups.

Part Two – 1994 to 1998 - Listening to the Practitioners

With the Men's World Cup coming to Sydney and to Australia for the first time and the appointment of Atlanta and America as the site for the 1996 Olympics, it was evident that the sport of hockey was on show to the New World. No more smoky back rooms in freezing Euro winters, the game was to be exposed to all in the open air. The new century was just around the corner, and how hockey presented itself in these dying years of the 20th would really be a foretaste for the new 21st century. Hockey needed a catalyst, a trigger point for change during these remaining five or six years. The hockey rulings of officials were still beset by political manoeuvring on committees more intent on seeing the world on the good ship F.I.H than getting on with the job of not just safeguarding the game, but projecting it into the new millennium as an all encompassing dynamic sport.

Could the average viewer really understand obstruction, the aerial ball and range of tackling allowed or whistled out? Indeed who could comprehend the appointment system at major tournaments which would leave a lone technical delegate in charge of appointing the Umpires for each match, and there were often over thirty of them in ten days?

The trouble at this stage was that no one was pushing a modern agenda that would be listened to seriously by the Rules Board. The same personnel rolled out the same agenda with an invincibility proven over the previous two decades.

Then it all kicked off!! Two Australian journalists at the World Cup were fighting in the press room to secure the one remaining seat at certain post match press conferences. They and their editors were anxious to listen to the comments of a World Cup Coach, which were mandatory straight after competition. That outrageous coach was not boring everyone silly with the "game of two halves" twaddle in comfortable middle class tones. Here was a blue collar lad exposing to the audience's delight the nocturnal activities of the F.I.H. Umpires party scene. Celebrations ran well into the night at the Darling Harbour Hotel whilst the players slept soundly in their beds, well prepared for the next day's matches.

There existed a double standard. It was unheard of for a mere Head Hockey Coach to in any way criticise the off the field preparations of officials and the Technical Delegate. This upstart, a former International Captain himself, even challenged the F.I.H. procedures of Umpires arriving at the World Cup only twelve hours before their first game the next day, having travelled halfway across the world from Europe. More hilarity followed his comments on playing in front of empty Aussie stands in the middle of the day at temperatures over 100 degrees. His classic comment, "Only mad dogs and Englishman play in the midday sun", brought the house down in mocking his fellow countrymen.

The F.I.H. organisation of old school Umpires presenting themselves in readiness for the tournament whenever they were allowed off work back at home, was laid open for all to see as farcical as umpire after umpire were complaining of heatstroke. One game, quite against protocol between India and South Africa was temporarily halted as players were forced to take drinks with just six minutes to play at the insistence of the South African Doctor. The game had started at 11:00 in the morning!

The attendances, the December heat, the officiating umpire booze-ups and the failure of the 1994 Men's World Cup to capture the sports-mad Aussies' imagination were there for all to see. Why did it take one individual coach to highlight this farce of a World Cup being officiated by umpires who clearly had formed a well rooted cultural clique?

One such umpire in his last tournament, who performed so poorly according to the Technical Delegate, that he was therefore given a bottom four playoff game, refused to umpire it, and walked out in disgust and returned home early to Europe.

This type of exclusiveness permeated umpiring at this time and was soundly exposed by the renegade coach of a nation that had competed very strongly at the World Cup. Was he supported by his fellow coaches? Not a hope, as coaches, like umpires, less than two decades away, were firmly in the control of National Chief Executives and Presidents who were more concerned about gaining positions on F.I.H. committees than in bringing in the age of a professional reality to hockey.

Naturally the F.I.H. closed ranks but there were some luminaries within its sprawling structure. No reaction appeared in the short term, but without doubt, a brave Umpire Coach at that tournament had also pinpointed the same observations with positive firm proposals for the future. Surely we no longer would have a solitary Technical Delegate deciding in a fair but sentimental manner which games would be umpired by which umpires. The late Graham Nash of many Olympics fame had pulled a flanker by withdrawing from selection as an umpire for the Atlanta 1996 Games. This was heresy, but the mark of true integrity and dynamism.

The F.I.H. responded!! They appointed Graham to be in charge of the umpires in Atlanta and it was he, once on site, who as the Umpires' Coach, would select the panel of umpires' suitability for every one of the matches. If you umpired well, you were there for seven matches: if you did not, you might get only two!! As with the players' selection, for the first time in umpiring a true meritocracy was being formed in Atlanta, Georgia where the first semblance of video technology to assist umpires was being seriously introduced.

The Spain vs. Holland Men's Final was umpired by the proven Aussie Don Prior and the rapidly emerging Ray O'Connor from, of all places, Ireland. The days of the domineering Latin set from France, Italy, Spain and Argentina as the cream of the non-aligned umpires were heading for a close, and therefore it is well worth tracing Ray's triumph at this level, because right across the world, these new procedures were about to be put into place at school, club and national competition status in men's and women's hockey. Was it a new dawn? I asked Ray,

"It took eight years from my debut at a tournament in Scotland to gain the recognition I felt I had deserved. I witnessed from 1987 preferential selections on an international basis, and long term sentiment tended to dominate umpiring appointments. Back when the long awaited and welcomed, by many, fitness tests were applied, there were still malingerers within the system who were catapulted to the fore. Was there an "us and them" mentality prior to 1994? Most definitely this was the case with umpires of little quality experience within their own nation often performed alongside officials who had seen better days. Agendas varied, consistency needed to be applied.

I was lucky to have been paired up with some rising stars during this period like Pete Von Reth, and began to really understand two vital elements of umpiring. First of all, Umpiring was not about decision-making".

"How can you possibly say that?!" I retorted.

"No, hear me out, it was all about knowing the game. If you knew what was really going on out there between the players, blowing the whistle was the easy bit. Yes, the rules had to be known and applied, but true umpiring started for me at this level when you appreciated why, when, and how play developed, indeed as you yourself have written, 'ruled by the play'. How often did I debate the theme with like minded umpires that possession of the ball was not necessarily advantage! Debate was commonplace during these years as there was little use of video playback to reinforce any learning experience from the F.I.H. In fact the only revelation was in the form of a 1989 video tape entitled 'Hockey for Umpires' and that was made by an independent hockey coach!!

Seriously, as good as that was, we were seldom helped in a mentoring capacity, and that was the way it was at every subsequent level. That perhaps explains why I learned to place so much emphasis on working as a pair both as an umpire, and as an Umpires Manager in selecting umpires later in my career. If you observe carefully hockey at any level, two brilliant but detached umpires would always be bettered by slightly weaker technicians, but a pair that had mastered the art of joint visual communication and game understanding, and that was all before earpieces!

I am certain that this was the reason that after nearly a decade I was to get my first Olympic final with the Australian Don Prior in Atlanta in 1996. Like a pair of twin strikers we anticipated every move, maybe we were frustrated players, but we read where the play was intended to go at any one time, and really allowed it to fruition or breakdown. Umpiring was becoming not an individual pastime but a team game. For the first time I heard from Graham Nash the expression that we were a team of Umpires, almost if you like, the thirteenth squad at a tournament. Yet, we were still a squad that had its own set standards, but very much working alongside the competing twelve"

Ray O'Connor on merit enjoyed a career which took in 178 Test matches, two World Cups, and two Olympic finals as well as officiating at five Champions Trophies. His story was another true example of the hockey dynamic at work, as he was very much part of the 'Listening years' as a top World Umpire and Umpires Coach. He was not only subject to the changing face of officialdom but actively pursued this evolution in umpiring with the likes of Pete Von Reth, Don Prior and the young John Wright of South Africa. By 1996, Ray and Don had umpired the last match where offside was still on the statute books! 'Times they were a changing' for sure when the Rules Board set up an Advisory Panel comprising Brigadier Atif from Pakistan, Roger Self of GB, Richard Aggiss of Australia and Alain Renaud of France. They were headed up by Roger Webb of England as Chairman to produce a template for the future of hockey, its rules and interpretations. Just to achieve this was momentous even though the Board duly rejected nearly all of their proposals!!

These human interactions were always to be criss-crossed by political agendas, but at last the great leaders in playing, coaching, management and umpiring were sitting together under an F.I.H. banner at the same table to talk sense, and eventually to implement their ideas onto a game that had been ready for change for some time.

The days of the Umpiring dynamic had duly arrived! Nevertheless, the question remained what could and would propel the game forward on all levels, and the answer was in the realms of technology and experimentation.

Part Three - Technology and Experimentation

There was no doubt that innovative Umpiring figures like Bob Davidson and Richard Kentwell from the western world of Holland and United States had patiently worked behind the scenes throughout this time period to bring new ideas to the physical fitness and overall preparation of umpires at top level tournaments. Bob, indeed, had introduced fitness testing as early as the Europa Cup of 1983 and Richard had pioneered the potential of video technology through his own distribution company. Both men knew the answer at all levels of hockey lay within the umpiring fraternity consulting with the players to bring about a more mutually understood game.

By the beginning of the new century, just over a decade ago, Umpiring lagged behind the coaching of players in the use of self assessment through video analysis. Club teams at national tournaments, and of course at international level, were all filming games to improve individual and team performance. Yet, with some exceptions, this was not broadly the case in how Umpiring Committees had worked within nations. All too often the standards of officiating were held back by self appointed Umpiring Committees that were too interested in regulating levels or badges of attainment rather than producing concrete materials and training for younger umpires in house, and at base level.

In short, any expertise within the international fold had not been handed down through the ranks in any tangible form in many of the developed nations of Europe, the Americas and Australasia with absolutely no attention to detail in visual form in Africa or Asia. Yes, it was the dawn of Umpires coaching and management, but overall there needed to be a cross-over transition of the use of video technology to assist the development of umpires and to explain a new era of rule changes by more modern forms of communication. A picture can show a thousand words! This must have been particularly disappointing for the one Aussie of the Umpires Advisory Panel, Richard Aggiss. An ex-international player and formidable coach to Australia, he stood as a well respected figure that even in that group provided a perfect bridge between the politically motivated Europeans, and the Asian representatives who were notably resistant to change. Richard had been a driving force in F.I.H. level coaching throughout the 1980's and had maintained a balance of true admiration for Asia style hockey, while still fascinated by the new developments within Europe.

This was much harder to work than it sounds as he had to contend with Army Brigadiers, Police Chiefs and representatives from the entrenched hierarchies of Asia that always regarded the Europeans with great suspicion especially when it came to game rule changes and tournament modification in scheduling. Peter Von Reth who later served enthusiastically on the F.I.H. Umpiring Committee commented,

"I cannot remember a time when Brigadier Atif appeared at any of the meetings. He often sent a cover person, like former Pakistan Captain, Isla-huddin. The net result was that we could never finalise a proposal as it had to go back for approval from Atif as the Chairman. All this did was to delay, water down, or even postpone our measures as we became frustrated, and were viewed as a mere talking shop. Asia, when it came to Umpiring, just was not prepared to experiment or implement as it always looked at every issue through continental eyes, and not from a hockey perspective."

This noted lack of co-ordination between the Rules Board, the F.I.H Umpir-ing Committees and the Continental Federations played a significant role in restricting any progress as it just took too much time to get anything through these enlarged committees. Just like in 1989, when Gavin Feath-erstone's 'Hockey for Umpires' video training tape was produced, it was individual enterprise that was pushing at the edges. Inconceivable it was that after a further eight years that groups of Umpires would meet before an F.I.H. Champions Trophy in Adelaide when Don Prior would at least in-troduce a series of clips from his Sport-Code facility to prepare the Umpires for readiness at that tournament. Don had a professional interest in offer-ing the scope of his expertise and enterprise, having already experimented with work in presentation form with Aussie Rules Football.

Only at the Utrecht 1998 World Cup for Men and Women did any essen-tial structured video coaching appear, but this was the direct result of the plentiful video feed that was available to all the National teams. Even then, it was a loose collaboration between the Umpires, often headed up by an Umpires Manager who had little professional acumen to provide structured video feedback for analysis. By the turn of the century hockey was still fragmented in every sense. Television had dabbled at the Majors, playing standards were rising disproportionately in the developed world as it embraced the advantage of advanced technology but still Umpiring was lacking overall planning and concerted leadership.

One early experiment involved the use of a full pitch video recording, al-lied to a second camera trained specifically onto one of the umpires. The latter was reproduced in the top left hand corner of the screen simultane-ously shown, while the overall play was screened. Its purpose was to show, in close-up, the reaction of the umpire to situations, with his subsequent signals and decision, and notably how he worked with his partner umpire.

Again, it was Graham Nash who was the Umpires Manager there at the Commonwealth Games in Manchester in 2002 that initiated such an idea in order to provide coaching to individual umpires between matches. Did

Graham have the video expertise? No, he just approached Gavin Feather-stone to conduct seminars at the tournament for both the coaching and umpires courses. Hockey was not wealthy, but at last it was starting to make use of the professional contacts within the sport. Here was deliberately built a bridge between the amateur and the professional, but it still was only constructed by hockey luminaries like Graham Nash.

There was a general consensus that a deteriorating situation, when compared to football and rugby, was developing as a result of hockey's complex set of rules. The laws of the Game were too complicated and not accessible to the general public. There still existed too many fouls and interruptions with the resultant lack of flow, open play goals and excitement in the game. More importantly, very few, repeat, few were looking at the game in an interconnected manner. For instance, it was no good The Rules Board with the Umpiring Committee's advice, tampering with one rule if it was going to backfire with respect to its effect on the spectators' point of view.

Over the most recent decade there had been wholesale changes and amendments to the sport's rules (more on this later) but where did all this come from? First of all, hockey umpiring had to come quickly into the 21st Century, and with the greater dialogue on the F.I.H Committees this definitely resulted in an atmosphere of experimentation.

"Let's try that out", was a common maxim, and with the world connected electronically, feedback through websites, the internet and an ever increasing movement of players, umpires and officials, meant that the old days of distance and delay tactics were a thing of the past in implementing new initiatives.

Genuinely, more practitioners like Peter Von Reth, Don Prior, Clive McMurray and Ray O'Connor were moving into influential positions and steering new interpretations on how hockey could be umpired. Individuals at last were making a difference. Still, in the rules, the Obstruction law was to be viewed differently, freedom for hit ins, roll on and roll off substitutions, and the beginnings of a more flexible approach to 3D skills (the lifting of the ball off the surface) all reflected 'the listening years' of F.I.H. officialdom.

However, as we will see, the hockey dynamic was even more radical than that! There were rumblings in Amsterdam, and as with many new collective initiatives the Dutch were at the forefront. As Peter Von Reth explained,

"We were now well into the 21st century, and as the Rules Board was essentially merging into the Umpires Committee of the F.I.H. we saw the need for more modern umpiring improvement on and off the pitch. It was vital to engage the two umpires as a pair so we introduced ear pieces to have games properly co-ordinated. At all levels we encouraged pre- tournament briefings firstly for the Umpires Managers with the umpires, and then with the Managers of competing teams. We reviewed areas of the game to stimulate more flow for the player and for the entertainment of the spectator. Most important was our desire to make changes that could be implemented at every level of hockey, a fact that many still do not quite appreciate"

Whether Mauritz Hendricks and Jos Hensel in 2005 appreciated it or not, they would introduce even more radical measures. They were at the thinking stage only then, as they would need a platform that would take in all their hockey dreams. Mauritz had been a very successful club coach with Jos as his strategic and commercial partner at Amsterdam Hockey Club, even when Mauritz moved onto coaching the Dutch National team earlier in the decade.

They saw the build up of frustration in the existing Men's and Women's European Club Competition played at the end of spring each year. Contested at a host club, a format that had existed for over three decades, it seldom attracted the potential interest it deserved with Holland/Germany finals repeatedly, low attendances, lack of Television and a poor return for any sponsors. The tournament fell within the remit of the European Hockey Federation, which desperately needed an 'adrenalin rush'.

So, by 2006, the European Hockey League (EHL) was born. Within this chapter, we will stick within the realm of how this dynamic uniquely changed the rules and how the game was played. Set against a reforming spirit within the F.I.H., certainly in European umpiring, there existed a pioneering feel within the autumn group games, and particularly in the final eight at the play-offs in the Netherlands in the spring. Peter again noted:

"There was no real problem for the E.H.L. to use a variety of changes and amendments in this competition. Indeed, we almost saw it as an unofficial arena for experiment as its organisers placed a new vision for hockey that would be more spectator friendly and televisual. The games were beamed live throughout Europe with the Finals attracting large crowds at the venues. What had they come to see?

Less whistle, more goals and high excitement were on the agenda as the 'self-start' free hit was introduced alongside the collection of high balls above the shoulder, and the novelty of the shave tackling from behind the line of the ball, meant more pace and committed action across the field. Structurally the matches with roll on, roll off substitutions were split into four quarters of 17½ minutes each. The tempo was relentless."

The action inside the Dutch stadia in Rotterdam and Amsterdam was placed onto large screens to record instances with the added excitement of the new third umpire in the stands calling on circle disputes. Drawn games at the knockout stages were decided not by the static penalty stroke, but by the advent of 1 versus 1 against the goalkeeper from the 25 yard line inside a time limit of 8 seconds. Jos and Mauritz had hit on a winner through their liberalisation of the rules. Games flowed with many more goals, and anyone who saw the matches for the first time would have been impressed by the freedom that the players were enjoying in the game. Even the umpires were stars as the E.H.L. took in an integrated image of player, umpire, coach, and spectator. Everything had cascaded down from these changes in the rules and interpretations to provide an exhibition for the possible future of hockey.

Now Euro Clubs adjudged themselves by qualifying for the E.H.L, and without doubt, it indirectly added the impetus in attracting top overseas playing stars from Australia, India, New Zealand and Argentina. The F.I.H Umpiring Committee looked on with baited breath as the competition took hold in the second decade of the new millennium. The third phase was presented on a plate for them as they travelled on a parallel line with the "Euro experiment". They literally could take on board from the tournament that which was popular, but notably, could be applied to the base level of junior and adult hockey across all the continents.

Noted Peter von Reth:

"That was the challenge as we debated what could and could not be applied globally. The frequency of our meetings on the Umpires committee was now coming through every year as we were under pressure to follow through with these new experiments, a far cry from the once every four year assessments of the past. I was comfortable in being part of that whilst the radical proposals were coming from within hockey itself.

There were so many areas to consider. Just take the example of the time structure of the game. Many matches worldwide are conducted on the basis of a hired facility. Until now a 1½ hours at schools and club level accommodated a warm-up and halftime. With an extra period as a break, and if games run to the shootout stage, suddenly two hour slots would be required and the clubs would have to undertake a 25% increase in the match costs.

Equally the shave tackle was discussed at length as it demanded an exact and precise level of timed execution. Slightly out, and injuries could certainly be a consequence. The same might apply for the ball being assertively played above the shoulder. Danger was always an element here and formed the base of many of our discussions.

Do not forget, I was part of the group that initiated the third umpire concept at first, we proposed it mainly as a means whereby the technology allowed us to make decisions on line debates. i.e. had the ball crossed the goal line?, was the shot inside the circle?, or was the tackle in or outside the 25?

We had no intention to go "tennis" with appeals and referrals, whereby the umpiring pair's decisions would be supported or overturned by the third umpire on an interpretation of any contested foul in the circle.
Since 2012, this trend has gathered apace to such an extent that at top tournaments now, the players will be standing still for over thirty minutes from a 60 minute game with all the quarter breaks and appeals and referrals. When will the game be allowed to flow again!?"

Peter has a valid point with just that one example which reflects an Umpiring Committee at F.I.H. level that is losing touch with the heartbeat of the sport. There are more examples of the artificiality of new rules like the recent proximity to the Circle 5 yard mobility free hit, and even more so, with the crazy long corner where attackers first must go and retrieve the ball outside the field and then throw it back onto the pitch at the point it exited to the 25 yard line. By this time all eleven players will nicely be set in defensive positions to deal with the "free hit". Where is the advantage? The flow? Like the offside rule of years before, the F.I.H. should not tamper with the long corner, but abandon it! Like indoors, it merits a free-out!

The hockey world is telling the F.I.H. to tone down interfering with the rules every year. It is confusing, and though many changes have been well received, too many as above, and like the own-goal experiment have not taken account the implications on the game as a whole. So, why all these changes, so regularly?

The answer is a sinister one, actually born out of a decision of the International Olympic Committee in 2013 to review five sports in danger of losing their Olympic status. Hockey was one of those sports. For sometime the I.O.C. have wanted to trim their numbers and 24 teams with officials, as hockey offers the current Games, falls into the category of too many, for too few medals, despite a century long tradition as a five ringed favourite.

To the I.O.C., accessibility and inclusivity are the key words that provide opportunity for all five continents to share in the winning of those coveted medals. For some time now, the Netherlands, Germany, and Australia have won the Lion's share of the medals over the last two decades. Money and technology, allied to western acumen has been the continual winner.

Recently overheard at the 5-a-side Junior Olympics was a comment from one of the I.O.C.'s highest, to an F.I.H. leading light,

"This is the future for you, it is accessible, cheap, and anyone can win"

The F.I.H. changes its playing rules like babies change nappies, because it is being squeezed by those above. Naturally the latter are invisible international sports politicians open to all types of persuasions and influences. They equally are subject to pressure groups from varied types of origins. For our game to survive, our international organisation must stand firm as a great global sport and be proud of its heritage, diversity and achievements.

Right down to our Umpiring Committees, they have got to realise that with every rule change, they are putting another nail in the hockey coffin as these decisions will be used against us as evidence that the sport is not happy within itself. Football and Rugby have seldom changed as team sports, so the F.I.H. must be resolute, and if any changes have to be made, let them be from our own hockey communities and not from marketing moguls and temporary sports politicians who are hardly worth two a penny.

*Umpires Ray O'Connor (Ireland) and John Wright (South Africa)
at the 2004 Olympics in Athens*

*Germany v The Netherlands -
A packed house for Monchengladbach, the border town*

-Part J-
Hockey's Risk Takers

For three young hopefuls, 1996 was to be the year the floodgates would be opened on their unfulfilled hockey careers. They had waited, oh yes, they had patiently waited for many years to make their respective contributions to the hockey dynamic. The trouble was, they were born and raised in the Republic of South Africa. The apartheid government had isolated its sportsmen and women from international competition since 1970 by its internal policy of racial segregation.

Now at the dawn of Olympic year in Atlanta in America's South, Sherylle Calder, Wayne Diesel and Craig Livingstone were poised to participate in the world's greatest theatre of dreams as all were due to be part of the South African hockey team. Their year stretched ahead of them with Sherylle captain of the women's team, Wayne as hockey's own head physiotherapist, and Craig as Assistant Coach to the men's group.

It had been a hard and record breaking road to Atlanta as the South African men had won both the All-African Games in Harare along with the Africa Cup in 1995 and '96. That was the simpler bit as the sport had to meet the South African Olympic Committee's requirement of a top 10 world ranking and more poignantly, had to satisfy the same powers that they were diversifying the playing personnel by inclusivity in player selection.

The enterprising President of S.A. hockey, Steve Jaspan, had hired a rebellious Englishman to deliver the goods and achieve a top 10 ranking in their return to International hockey at the Sydney World Cup with the old boys. Then, the real challenge, Gavin Featherstone as Head Coach had to revamp the squad into a more youthful, and more inclusive content to retain that position in Atlanta. It was the first hockey Olympics that South Africa was to play in for forty years.

Yet, South Africa was hungry for participation and success. It was only that year in '95 that Nelson Mandela had worn the Springbok shirt to win the Rugby World Cup and Bafane-Bafane had won the football Africa Cup of Nations. The country was abuzz on sport, and the Rainbow Nation was desperate to introduce its talent on and off the field onto the world stage.

So along came the three to offer their varied abilities to the Olympic party. As so often occurs in life, it was not quite to go to plan in the short term. For Sherylle, the composed central defender of South Africa for many years, and then in her twilight years, Atlanta would be the last throw of the dice. She had grown up speaking Afrikaans in her native Bloemfontein in the Orange Free State despite her original Scottish name. The girls had also won the All-Africa Title, but had to win the Olympic Qualifier to be held in Cape Town at the turn of the year in order to qualify.

They did not qualify, to her anguish. The best part of two decades blown away in nine days, her Olympic dreams shattered in the shadow of Table Mountain at Hartleyvale. What was she to do now with her life as she announced her subsequent retirement? The answer will be revealed in these papers, but suffice to say, she singly transformed an area of sports science that was to have a tremendous influence on world sport in and beyond hockey.

Meanwhile the Hockey Boks had taken on two sharp characters in Wayne and Craig to assist the well travelled Englishman. Both had through residence or education a broad experience of working in South Africa's contrasting states of Transvaal, the Free State and Natal. Yet, as a result of further education respectively in Medicine and Law, it was Wayne and Craig's intent to follow both family and professional life in the nation's commercial hub of Johannesburg in the Transvaal.

Not unlike many young aspirants, they had attached their early working lives to law and medical practices which would lay the foundations for their future astounding successes in hockey and beyond. Ironically, Craig was a talented provincial player ready to rise up the coaching ranks during the lean years, whilst Wayne ominously enough, preferred to kick footballs around in his leisure time!! They had another thing in common, a true desire to reach the top in their chosen field.

As with Sherylle, the question was, would it be in this Atlanta Olympic year that it would all happen for them?

The women's team captain was now out of that equation, but Craig and Wayne would play their part in a very creditable South African men's' performance to finish in the top 10 with draws against Korea and Australia and two players voted as the most exciting young players of the Games in Greg Nicol and Brian Myburgh.

For an introduction back into international sport with the youngest team and youngest coaching and medical staff, Livingstone and Diesel had every reason to be satisfied with their Olympic work.

Gavin Featherstone had done his troubleshooting job in placing the Hockey Boks into the big time in just three years and he parted company with his bosses after Atlanta, but what of our favoured three? Where did hockey leave our "Class of '96"? All were fascinated by the contributions that one could broadly associate with Sports science, where their specific academic qualifications met headlong with not just hockey, but sport in general. So, would they be in or out? Would they remain in the sport that had encouraged their rise or spread their wings?

They were all lateral thinkers and rather than get exposed to the ruthless world of international playing competition, they sought out avenues whereby they could influence the game and sports at all levels. Equally they were innovators in their approach to sport, and internationalists that recognised the broad platform that top level sport had become in its development in that decade.

Whilst others ploughed a narrow funnel, all three were prepared over the ensuing years to become world travellers with Wayne effectively emigrating with his family to Britain, whilst both Sherylle and Craig shuttled back and forth between continents. Significantly, the former used his thorough knowledge of his medical field in sports science to principally football, whereas Sherylle and Craig's clients would entail a very wide base in sport. Flexibility was king in their every move.

At this juncture, it is vital to summarise the sporting environment into which these three dynamic characters would throw their energies over the next twenty years up until today. Both on a world and local scale the team games of rugby and hockey had gone professional, not just at international level, but also in offering individuals the opportunities to cross borders to seek out a living by competing at club status. This expansion would have applied to playing and coaching roles, and many at later stages in their careers took advantage of the player-coach scenario as a furtherance of their expertise.

In football, the English Premier League had evolved in 1992 out of the original Football League and Europe followed in their steps with La Liga in Spain, the Bundesliga in Germany and Serie A in Italy. What really mattered here was the Television rights to relay the broadcasts all over the world with the subsequent staggering revenues. Add to this that we were entering the digitised era of telecommunications. It all meant that the sporting world had been transformed as a commercial entity as globalisation gripped the world by the end of the century.

As little from then on was a sporting secret anymore with intrusive cameras and the ever increasing number of TV and radio stations devoted specifically to one sport, the margins for competitive success became narrower and narrower. The often quoted line that games were won and lost on tiny percentages of preparation was certainly gaining force as teams like Manchester United would steal away with a European Cup Final triumph over Bayern Munich in the last two minutes with two goals.

In an earlier chapter, the role of video introspection was reviewed, but suffice to say here that it was providing the smallest details for analysis for sporting managers at all levels. Arsene Wenger had at Marseilles and Arsenal pioneered new methods of training on and off the field, and had been responsible for introducing specialised diets for his players to achieve peek energy levels for the weekend matches. The days of a pie and a pint were well gone!

The sporting world that Wayne, Sherylle and Craig had stepped into in 1997 was exactly the work that was to suit their skills, initiative and driving personalities. As my American colleagues would say, they were a perfect fit. Cometh the hour, cometh the dynamic. The world was to be their oyster!!

Wayne Diesel

Wayne Diesel left the message at the White Hart Lane reception desk and all it revealed was the invitation for a meeting at the Enfield training ground on the Monday morning at 7am. Anyone who knows London and the M25 will appreciate that this made some sense in order to avoid the teeming masses of rush hour. For me, it was an eccentric time, but for the head of Medical Services at Tottenham Hotspur Football Club, it was just another day at the office. He had to face the journey from Croydon, the furthest southerly point of M25 London to arrive at Enfield, the furthest northerly point every single day. That indeed was life in London in 2014.

I met my former physiotherapist, now sporting a 'Spurs' tracksuit like the other 20 employees starting their working day at this ungodly hour. He welcomed me into the light of the giant purpose-built training centre building in strict contrast to the outside dark of a late November morning.

"Geeze, great to see you again Gav, after all these years", he beckoned me inside.

"The last time I came to Tottenham's training ground we, Chelsea Apprentices, lost 5-1 and Graeme Souness was playing!!" was my reply.

"Let me show you around the place", Wayne boasted.

The basic structure of the new build was a straight lined 'U' shape with the two long sides of the 'U' corresponding separately to the Academy/Development wing, the other to the first team sector. The base of the 'U' was the administrative end upstairs with an array of pools, specialised rooms and the medical centre downstairs. The space inside the 'U' was a 70 by 50 yard rubber crumb synthetic surface with accompanying football training aids.

This was all 21st century high technology in practice. The separate wings were very significant here at Tottenham, as they exuded almost a class system within the Hotspur whole. Initially I was shown the Academy sector with its orthodox tiled walls and pristine carpets. Hanging from the walls were action photos of young Academy players that had made the grade, the one in the middle was of Harry Kane, the current centre striker for Spurs and the England U21 team. We moved between changing rooms that had surpassed any of my career's hockey facilities for the clubs seven age group squads. These days they started them as the U9's gravitating up to the Apprentices aged 16 and over.

Outside were superbly manicured football fields where the old art of groundsmanship still held true for the fortunate few to play at this level every winter Saturday morning. The previous Saturday I had witnessed the schoolboy U15 squad performing, and the memories came flooding back. Watched by two dozen sets of parents who had breezed through the security gates, and playing under the watchful eye of a bevy of former professional players, the two teams responded well and there were still many parallels from my glory days at Chelsea. I knew what they were going through.

The intensity was still there, the kids were playing for Tottenham, the beginning of a football dream. Yet, you could see even at this level, the boys were conscious of their own every move as there was an individualism that pervaded through the team ethic. They were desperate to show their worth, seemingly in the knowledge that of the sixteen out there playing that day, that maybe, just maybe, one of them might make it into the big time at Tottenham.

155

It is hard to express to the outsider what goes through a young footballer's mind at this tender age. He is partially aware early in life that this is his big chance with many of the boys coming from deprived neighbourhoods with little or no education. The world seems to weigh on his shoulders. If he fails to make it, he feels he has let down his mum and dad, his street, his school, his mates, everyone.

Back inside, even with the young ones at Tottenham, there would be additional rooms, study rooms. Whatever their academic background, they were to be encouraged to work through their national exams whilst at the club. Notably once signed on as an Apprentice, they had to realise some academic potential where GCSE and Advanced level school exams were there to study as a challenge. At Chelsea in 1969, a GCSE/O level pass in one subject by a player was an exception with the unsuspecting individual having to live it down and being dubbed with the nickname, 'Prof'!

Wayne Diesel was now to show me through the doors that led to the First Team wing and medical centre. First of all, I was trained to notice carpets, as suddenly I felt as if there was an extra layer under my feet as we walked through the corridors of the exalted First Team sector. Even the tiles on the walls had changed with an upgrade of specification depicted by new elaborate patterns.

We moved into Wayne's den. The rehabilitation pool of prescribed depths and temperatures for hot and cold recovery sessions was in evidence and then into the fitness testing suite and the plyometric area for muscular development. There was no evidence of free weights, just weight-bearing machines to absorb the muscular tension. Wayne introduced me to the humidity suite where players literally could lose pounds in body mass, if required, by wearing a specially designed quadruple layered body suit. Then we entered a chamber which challenged the author's breathing capacity. The sports medicine man with the turn of a dial had reduced the oxygen in the room by 20%, one of the prerequisites for building up cardiovascular efficiency.

The aim of this Centre was to keep the fit as healthy as was possible and to enhance fast and effective recovery from injury and illness. It was a 'Smorgasbord' of scientific aids to enhance performance and to stimulate the body's response by artificially presenting harsh conditions. In short, it was a time saving arena to hasten recovery by qualitative medical means. Within these walls you could achieve maximum physical ability without journeying to different climates, altitudes or other restrictive elements. Rather like in a hospital, all the players' results from physical testing were monitored by Wayne and his staff as each individual player progressed through the nine month season.

There was also an evolutionary path where Wayne had assured me that his staff's ideology was to build physical performance by concentration on the fit and healthy. As opposed to the past, when the medical teams would spend 80% of their weekly time attempting to get two players with chronic injuries fit to play with only a 30% yield in match time.

Quality oozed from such an environment. Whoever was the manager and coaching staff, and Wayne had outlasted five bosses in his eight years at Tottenham, they had the kind of backroom support that could only be envied by many National Sports Associations.

An example of this was how the Tottenham medical staff had dealt with the near tragedy of Fabrice Muamba who had collapsed as a Bolton Wanderers midfielder while playing at White Hart Lane during the 2012 season. Wayne had always previously recognised the services of the St. John's Ambulance provision, but early on he had insisted only on having trauma-experienced medical staff pitch-side at matches who had worked at scenes of motorway accidents and other life threatening situations.

That decision was crucial on that day as the Tottenham staff were placed under extreme pressure at the time of the player collapse. In effect, Patrice's heart had stopped for a full 50 minutes. The crowd silenced as the severity of the situation was realised with Wayne having to manage a life and death dimension. The ensuing tense minutes in front of 40,000 people as a player struggled for his life thankfully resulted positively, and the subsequent reaction of the day's spectators and the medical world in general was to rally behind all those associated with the Spurs medical team's actions that day.

Wayne Diesel, indeed, received plaudits from the highest points in the land, including formal recognition from the country's royalty. In my discussions with him, he typically never even mentioned the part he had played in the life saving scenario.

The grandstanding that we normally associate with such responsible positions in top sport simply went missing when it came to Wayne Diesel, and this very fact does give us a clue to his continuing professional success. Back in 1994, he was new to practicing his speciality in the International sport of hockey which commanded a great deal of world competition without the appropriate levels of publicity. It was a modest sport on a huge learning curve and he was very much part of that process,

"Gav, I learned so much in those hockey days in relation to how teams were prepared both prior to tournaments and during the amazing twelve days at World Cups and Olympic Games. I had a baptism of fire with respect to injury and the rehabilitation treatment of players who had to peak in seven matches in just that short period of time. I think there would be a worldwide football and rugby revolution if their World Cup players had to play within such a tight time scale. I do remember very well how many deadlines you used to set me in order to get injured players ready for the next tournament match".

Obviously with such professional attachment, it was a question of what really were the main reasons for such a hockey specialist to leave the sport altogether after the Atlanta games in 1996.

Wayne continued,

"Hockey provided me with all the basic experiences that I have drawn from throughout my career. Professionally the sport was evolving when I was involved, to where it is today, but back then I had already realised that I needed day to day challenges in the sports medical field. I had caught the bug of international sport, which only a fulltime professional position in sports medicine could offer me.

Along came the chance to work at the institute in Cape Town with South Africa's cricket team and three years later the opportunity to go international with England's Premier League Rugby Club, Gloucester.

With each successive move the conditions as far as professional medical progress was concerned just continued from good to excellent as technological advances were pushing sports medicine into the realms of advanced pro-active injury prevention. During this period I have been exposed to a broad scope of experiences in respect to the kinds of injuries I was dealing with in association with the varied sports of cricket, rugby and football. I literally treated players with major trauma conditions through to dealing with biomechanical variations in body type, to intricate assessments of finger and digital stress fractures which came with the challenges from these different sports. The real point was that I was at the centre of a results driven industry. Time was always of the essence and I was compelled to come up with the appropriate solutions, the tried and tested ways alongside new pioneering methods to combat and treat a whole range of injuries. In today's job interviews, this would all come under the heading of professional development, but development under pressure!

The physiotherapist's and chief medical officers were answerable to the high rollers, the Club Chairmen and managers. I enjoyed that pressure, because you could measure by your methods the success of individuals and team availability on the pitch. Training methods were set to specific requirements with individual connection to the players. Whilst hockey was at full stretch affording the new synthetic pitches all over the world, the sports of Rugby, Cricket and Football knew no bounds to costs as either governments, sponsors or millionaire benefactors came up with enormous investments. What did that mean? It represented a tight fusion between the medical and sporting world from separate training field provision and internal rehabilitation pools to scrimmaging machines and kicking coach specialists. In simple terms, these three sports had moved on to a new dimension that hockey just could not match in the material world.

Another factor that really took me away from hockey was not just this scope that other sports offered, but also the direction in which rugby and football, notably in England, had been heading. During this recent period one club could truly boast seven or eight differing international origins in one team. Both at Gloucester and then at Charlton Athletic, and even more so at Tottenham, I have been constantly administering fitness and injury assessments and have had to adapt my treatments often depending on the nationality and culture of the individual. For instance, some players here at Spurs insist in their treatments of conducting acupuncture and acupressure techniques, others in the area of diet simply refuse to take on board certain foods as a result of their cultural background.

The world faces you every day you come here to the training ground to work, and if you cannot learn, and learn quickly, you just do not survive as a player, medical practitioner, or even as the team manager! I have seen five managers here come and go in eight years covering four differing nationalities with hugely different football backgrounds and philosophies. Some, to my mind, were coaches, some were managers. English football seems to be split in two with the cult of the training ground coach forever working new practical ideas deeply contrasting with the player-centric manager who thrives around the more motivational side of inspiring and preparing his staff and teams.

Whoever you work with, they always want their players fully fit and ready for the next game. I know that I have never guaranteed this but the sport has taught me so much in terms of experience that today in 2015 I have become better equipped to recognise parallel conditions and injuries that I have faced before. That was always the case with hockey in my earlier days and I have come through that sport to recognise its essential differences to the pressures of everyday existence in England's Football Premiership. Hockey is a passion for many players and participants worldwide. The game brings the people together in the social realm to such an extent that I am regularly in contact with our 1996 South African Olympic Team.

Football never dwells on the social basis, my spare time involves 180 hours per year on seminars and conducting lectures on sports medicine topics all over the sporting world as medicine depends upon importing and imparting knowledge within its professional community. As for meeting football friends in a social context, it just does not happen these days. Our former Tottenham manager Harry Redknapp used to tell many anecdotes about times during his playing career at West Ham. One was:

'After any home game at West Ham, the word got out for all the first team boys to meet up at a succession of East End pubs for a Saturday night knees-up, sometimes the lads alone and other times with the wives and girlfriends. The boys were all local lads then, and they could go from one to the next blindfold!'

Those were the days in football, but hockey has retained some of that vital social element. In reality, it is built into its system and is vital for its continued success at all levels. It is because hockey has stayed that way that we are meeting, the two of us here today. I know that hockey was the trigger that launched me towards all my own sporting dreams."

Sherylle Calder

It was a dark evening that night in Sydney. The England Rugby Team had worked a line-out just minutes before the climax of the World Cup Final. Steve Thompson, the huge hooker, took the ball on the sideline, paused very carefully and launched the perfectly executed throw to the back of the line-out where, England won the ball whereby their tight forwards drove the extra ten yards toward the Australian line.

The diminutive scrum half, Matt Dawson eked out and organised the slow drive of the Pack for a precious few extra yards so they were within the distance radar of fly-half Jonny Wilkinson. Dawson collected and spun the ball, Wilkinson caught and transferred it for the drop kick between the posts from 30 yards. The rest is history, England were World Champions!

The well rehearsed move had been done one thousand times. Jonny Wilkinson never got bored with repetition, but neither did he ever down-play the role that Sherylle Calder brought to the England team throughout the preparations in 2003. Sherylle had discussed the move to Clive Wood-ward's England at a Stellenbosch vineyard over a very liquid lunch with the author of these pages just eleven months earlier. The net result meant that she was heading for the R.F.U. of England! There was a choice, but dis-counting the exclusivity of the New Zealand All Blacks, she never regretted the move as the launching pad for a glittering career as the 'Eye Doctor' of world sport.

To her, it was a million miles away from her upbringing in the sleepy capital of the Orange Free State, Bloemfontein, where as a young Afrikaans-speak-ing girl, she showed exceptional talent in the sport of hockey. The expres-sion of her abilities went unseen, as in her formative years at school and at her beloved Stellenbosch University, South Africa was deemed a rogue state with its separatist politics. This meant that a boycott prevented her from playing internationally right into her thirties. Even then, in her quest for knowledge and technical improvement she had the habit of appearing in Dutch Club hockey in the close seasons.

As a player and deep defender, there was a timelessness about her. All the great competitors have had it, the Franz Beckenbauers and Bobby Moores, of giving the impression that they had all the time in the world. Sherylle never seemed to sprint in any game. Something in her disposition seemed to sense the play about to happen. There was an awareness (a word we will return to), a positional control on her own movement in relation to the ball, her opponents and team mates that was uncanny.

Despite all this, South Africa's Women did not qualify for the 1996 Olympics and Sherylle formally retired from hockey, or had she?

"For some time during my international playing years, just the 3 of them, I had to pursue a path of self-assessment and analysis of what I brought to my individual game and the team as a whole. I was aware that I seemed to get to points of danger earlier than my fellow players and that I identified space very easily when I was active on the field. Was it, I asked myself, a natural gift of vision or just a result of the requirements of the central posi-tion that I was asked to play.

I initiated simple exercises to view the field better and for our players to become aware of the spaces around them. Without yet a scientific base, I was already working on my team mates, attempting to make all of us much more aware of what was transpiring around us. I was motivated by one aspect, and that was how I could transform my ideas on vision and space into the practical reality of improving technical skills."

Sherylle, not unkindly, had not been influenced unduly by any hockey coaches in South Africa. Indeed, coaching had almost understandably stagnated in the two decades of isolation from the hockey mainstream.

"You could as a player, either accept that situation and stagnate yourself, or you could reach out and explore the possibilities that were out there to enhance individual and team performance. My own reaction was to conduct research, gain a Doctorate in the academic arena and present papers that would thrust the multiple ideas I had into a scientific acceptance that the eye could be trained to bolster balance, peripheral awareness and the brain's ability to make considered decisions on the sports field."

She had made contact with Professor Tim Noakes at the Sports Science Institute, and during these years at the end of the century, insisted on securing an office for herself as the new facilities were instated at the University of Cape Town. The support from Morné du Plessis, a formidable ex-Springbok Rugby legend and from Tim Noakes, however, was a two-way street. They realised that Sherylle was treading new ground here in academic and scientific terms. For them, as for her, the element of risk was huge in this undertaking.

It was on her shoulders, in that she had to show through her Ph.D. in 1999 the validity of her science in theoretical, and eventually, more to the point, in practical terms. In the long term, Noakes knew that the exposure from Sherylle's work could reflect positively on his Institute. Note that the Institute itself was at a fledgling stage in its development. Nevertheless, Sherylle did find it heavy going in these early stages as she attempted to formalise her findings.

"By procedural means, I had to present my ideas, having attended Optometric Association Conferences, to a whole range of Optomologists. All these centres for study were focused in the United States, and there were eminent academics that would have to consider my thesis from Stanford and Harvard Universities.

The real opposition centred on the fact that I was extending the traditional boundaries of Optometry and promoting the theories that the eye could be trained to enhance sporting performance. In the end, my thesis was considered by six different academic experts and was finally taken up by the learned profession. My theoretical credentials were out there for all to see along with already established practical data. My research was

162

well founded at the Sports Science Institute, and I had a ready group of students in a variety of field sports that were ready and willing to test my theories.

Feedback was paramount, and we could measure the rate of individual improvement in players over a season's duration. I was able to assess an individual by checking his or her history in a cognitive sense, before conducting exercises and field training. The net result was one in which they improved their decision making with the ball, even through they often were presented with more diverse options. As they gained a greater sense of confidence in acquiring these qualities, it was commonplace to notice they were becoming more attuned to risk taking, and risk taking with successful outcomes. Many critics always used to argue that my research was confined to individual development rather than aimed at greater team efficiency. My experiences informed me that teams were often well rewarded as there was a build up of successful options and possibilities. Team mates would cross refer and notice the difference in shutting down weaknesses and accentuating strengths that helped to make the smooth running of the team."

Whether it was acuity in the eye, peripheral awareness, depth perception, or the ability to transfer all the eye to brain to skill process, it was a fact that word was getting out that Sherylle Calder the Eye Doctor was stimulating interest in her field amongst the highest practicioners in world sport.

One such leader who had the reputation of thinking outside the box was Clive Woodward, the England Head Rugby Coach. He himself had escaped Britain late in his international playing career to play for Manly Rugby Club in Sydney. This period of time was instrumental in his forming ideas and principles which in the future would take him to four 5 Nations Championships before 2003. Good enough as this was, the World Cup in Australia was the real target later that year.

Woodward constantly searched for the decisive edge in performance in adding a specialised kicking coach, and even a referee consultant to his staff to explain away Southern Hemisphere interpretations on both open play and set pieces. Yet, he wanted more, and with a brilliant Pack led by Martin Johnson, he still craved even more possession from scrums and in particular the line-outs. He had a talented kicker in Jonny Wilkinson, but this asset would have been negated if there was no guarantee of line-out ball after the fly-half had gained ground by his tactical kicking.

He had heard that Sherylle was offering fieldwork beyond the theories of how individual training on the eye could accelerate rugby skills, such as the fly-half and hooker estimating more consistently the distances, height, and trajectory of the ball necessary to gain full advantage. Sir Clive was to have the All Blacks as a major rival in investing in Sherylle's new science. Woodward had gauged her mood, and the stage she was at in her individual career. He was willing to give her flexibility in the work place, whilst the All Blacks demanded exclusive use of her findings.

The Cape Town Doctor had taken over five years to gain acceptance in the academic sphere to make the connection between the human eye and its association with appropriate sporting skills. In turn Sir Clive had recognised that Sherylle needed a platform to prove the practical application of her ideas. He gave her complete access to the England squad, but also encouraged her to be able to offer seminars in academic forums throughout the European Rugby world.

This English connection was different from her internal workings within South Africa with a selection of Springbok Netball, Football and National team cricketers. She was moving with her ideas, drills, and practical work into a world dimension. Was there a problem with an overseas woman formalising training in a very male macho sport like Rugby?

"No, never. The players I worked with undoubtedly knew that big international games were won on small margins, and they were hungry for anything that could tip their own performance to a new level. We worked intensively on ball distribution and in the throwing accuracy at line-outs and how the kicking at penalties could be that bit more precise"

Any English or World Rugby fan knows the impact that Jonny Wilkinson and Steve Thompson had made in these specialised areas of the game over a period of seven years. Both had the talents prior to Sherylle's nine month intervention but could they guarantee consistency under pressure? Judging from the move that led to Wilkinson's drop goal and his subsequent winning kick, the answers were obvious.

Will Greenwood, England's ace centre of the World Cup winning team certainly reinforces her contribution,

"Sherylle, diminutive in stature, ginormous in vision, be it introducing acronyms such as CTC or catching balls with eye patches on, she has her fingerprints all over the Webb Ellis Trophy alongside those of the players on the pitch. Brilliant lady to work with, and call a friend"

From the end of 2003, the offers poured in for Sherylle's expertise. They ranged from a struggling Ernie Els, who she helped to stage a great comeback to win the British Open, to pushing the training expansion on the Spanish hockey team goalkeepers, but also ironically to returning to South Africa to have full access to the Springbok World Cup Rugby team of 2007. Could she repeat another Rugby Gold medal using similar training methods?

Again the answer was in the positive as South Africa won the World Cup in their home country. As for Sherylle, her skills were to become a thriving business as she opened her Eye Gym in Cape Town, basing herself at the Stellenbosch Academy of Sport. Her professional development was made more systematic with further intricate software, and what was so vital, her flexibility to cross the world to encounter new sports enquires.

Her recent triumphs included the Olympic Gold medal for the Dutch hockey Women in London 2012, who affectionately dubbed Sherylle with the nickname 'Golden Eyes', and her direct involvement with the Formula One Williams Motor Racing team in the form of Valtteri Bottas, one of the fastest drivers in the world.

Perhaps as Sherylle takes her ideas into the corporate world with fresh enthusiasm, it is worth noting that she still is alive to what made things happen for her. She always appreciated the backing of the legendary Danie Craven as the first Man of Stellenbosch Sport, and how she was inspired by notable international hockey coaches who thought outside the box. Her story very much reflects that quality in herself, a single minded quest to acquire all the skills that contributed to greater performance.

In 1996, one such 'brother in arms', Ric Charlesworth, the hockey icon for Australia, came up with a novel idea to prepare his HockeyRoos for the forthcoming Olympic games in Atlanta. He had himself selected a Women's World XI to travel to sub-tropical Darwin in Australia to play a Series against his World Cup Champions. Suffice to say that Sherylle was the only South African selected, and later she was to state that this selection to his invited team was her highest playing honour in her career.

On departing from the humidity of Darwin after the week's completion, Ric handed out his latest written work on hockey to Sherylle and with it, a profound statement on the book's inside front cover, it said,

"Not taking a Risk is a Risk in itself."

Little did he know then, he was preaching to the converted!

Craig Livingstone

As a boy, Craig Livingstone would pack up his beef jerky and oranges and head off with his Dad to watch his beloved Natal play provincial rugby in what was then called the Currie Cup. This was the internal competition that kept South African rugby alive as it remained boycotted and isolated from world rugby. Meanwhile, he developed a keen interest at the equivalent level of hockey as a calm defensive midfield player.

Rugby, remember, was the religion, hockey a mere sport, but a sport that was social as well as competitive. The social dimension was also very close-knit and it was quite commonplace to develop friendships, rivalries and business connections with contemporaries that would last for life. In Craig's case, they would exist from as far afield as Cape Town, Pretoria and Johannesburg. These distances did not phase sporting competition, nor Craig as he competed in almost every South African province.

Still, it was rugby union, to this day, that inspired him the most in the same way that football had for Wayne Diesel and hockey had done for Sherylle Calder. Livingstone, a perfectly British name for Southern Africa, and in particular, the province of Natal, often described itself as the last bastion of the British Empire, was to play out his formative years in a very different province. He was to study Law at the Witwatersrand University in Johannesburg. Hockey apart, he would take a keen interest in the Contract Law course for his degree in the commercial hub of the country.

He was the type of individual who became increasingly frustrated by the sporting and political isolation, but he never stood still, acquiring invaluable playing and coaching awards, so that when the day came, he was ready and willing to play a formative part. That day was to arrive by 1993 when South African hockey was readmitted to international competition and was to qualify for the World Cup in Sydney in 1994.

South Africa needed a bridge between isolation and real international performance, and not being able to trust the limited experience of its native born coaches, it looked overseas for an impact coach, someone that could galvanise the available talents quickly. They found their man in Gavin Featherstone, but on the understanding that he would take on a young South African as his Assistant that would be groomed for a future in the nation's coaching hierarchy. Craig was that appointee.

It was a wise choice as the perceptive South African had a keen eye for detail with an unmistakably inquiring personality. His reading of the game was exemplary, but his willingness to learn the practical side of the game's tactical appreciation was even greater. He was aware that the missing years had made life difficult for all of the South African sports coaches starting off as international fledglings.

For Craig to understudy a well travelled international coach with all of his assets and deficiencies, was a learning experience as he, on the way, was exposed over just two years to the full diversity of hockey nations with their contrasting styles of play. South Africa's transition was truly an eventful one as the squad reinvented itself into the top 10 in the world whilst introducing a new generation of players. For the Head Coach, Livingstone's knowledge across the provinces was invaluable as he had, as a senior provincial player himself, competed with or against most of the top athletes.

He patiently observed his head coach fight the bruising battles, not against international opponents, but within the nation's antiquated selection committees, the new politicised masters inside the Hockey Association, and most of all, the racially aware South African Olympic Committee. Craig also now could assess an FIH structure that appeared to be commercially and economically well behind its field sport rivals of football, cricket and rugby union. Livingstone, a shrewd analyst at all times, took note with all this information not lost on him.

So how did he see the situation as he boarded the Rainbow Warrior 747 jet taking him back home from Atlanta in 1996 after the hockey team registered a top 10 finish with the youngest squad at the Games? He takes up the story,

"I did not see a future for myself in hockey. Although it had been an enjoyable and fulfilling experience, it was also a career defining one for me. I was not clear on hockey's future, fearing it would not progress as a result of the obvious lack of funding. The sport needed to be administered by a more commercially minded group of managers to run its organisation.

My impression following Gav's departure after Atlanta, was that the playing and coaching had far accelerated away from the administrative and management side of the sport. It had become a mismatch, partly due to South Africa's isolation, but also as a result of the intransigence of the provincial and national bosses in protecting their fiefdoms.

So I decided to take the leap into the business world of sport, using my legal background and my hitherto sporting contacts as an effective combination. The sporting climate was very delicate in 1996 as politically the new democracy was only two years old. Isolation had meant that we were very inexperienced in all aspects of sport and specifically in the professionalism required to succeed. I guess that what I attempted then was groundbreaking for South Africa.

I saw a gap in the market as Rugby had only just turned professional in 1995 and the close structure of links across the sports in Natal meant that I had known some of the Rugby coaches who introduced me to the players who needed legal advice for their prospective contracts."

The dynamic had clicked in, as Craig was the right person at the right time. His new company was thriving, and though he was not the first sports agent, he was certainly the premier one that had come totally from a hockey background. I asked him what qualities he had needed for his adopted role.

"Definitely needed to be calm and patient, but at the same time, to be outgoing as the players were 'commodities', and you were obliged to sell your client to the team, club or sponsor. You had to be confident in what or who you were selling and to understand the needs of top flight players and how they thought. I was lucky here that I had gone through that stage myself when coaching any team. It was and remains a life skill. At this stage, Rugby was the most relevant to the services I was offering, but remember, it was new territory for those involved in that sport as well. Expectations were low as the players were uncertain of what lay ahead, but they did know then, the most important task was to secure a solid contract."

Craig's background was to come up trumps because he was legally trained in Contract Law, had performed as a coach at world level, but just as essential, he knew what made a South African sportsman tick. His challenge was to effectively merge these three assets in the service he offered to clients who were entering a wide new world of competition. It was not, as you would imagine, as easy as that. There were obstacles, notably when the contracts became of an international nature, and particularly with certain sports. He continued,

"My main obstacles were the Rugby Unions at first, as they did not want to work through the agents. The agents that had been involved with football had rather jaundiced the industry as most of them were ex-professional players with no legal training whatsoever. The Unions tried to cut the agents out as they initially felt that, if they did not deal with an agent, they would get the player at a cheaper cost. In time, notably in rugby and cricket, the Unions realised the importance of an agent, as did the players."

Craig has continued his work mainly within the internal side of South African sport whereby Rugby can offer the Southern hemisphere's Super Club League which has pitted the best of the South African provinces against their Australian and New Zealand counterparts. Commercially he has taken advantage of the overseas markets for national rugby players, a very successful venture after the SA World Cup triumph of 2007, and had equal success in placing SA cricketers into the English county cricket championship and the high riding Football Premiership.

He claims his work has few examples from the modern world of hockey which, kind of reinforces his original decision to leave the sport nearly two decades ago. He still feels the sport could have been put on a professional footing, but suggests that until it becomes more TV friendly, it will still lag behind its competing field sports, despite its Olympic status. His Company awaits with interest how the current Indian Hockey League Franchise may take off against a cluttered background calendar of Olympics, World Cups, Indoor World Cups, Champions Trophies, Euro Hockey Leagues and domestic competitions. 'Too many cooks spoiling the broth?'

Craig Livingstone, very different to our two previous personalities, was a hockey coach. He viewed the situation in 1996 in the same way by taking a long and hard look at where he could most utilise his skills to realise his sporting potential. They all moved away from hockey.

They had all seen the direct results of isolation in South Africa, and, indeed, its short term toll on the transition period. In hockey, they had all been amateurs. Years of participation had passed with no recompense. Yet they saw the light at exactly the right time at the dawn of the digitised, and in rugby's and hockey's case, the outset of the professional era. Risk taking, normally frowned upon in the conservative hockey circles around the world, was to be their challenge, but they were more than ready to plunge headlong into their new ventures.

These three dynamic characters, all by-products of a political and sporting system, bucked the trend to pursue their individual lines of talent which had been nurtured through their early contact with hockey. What a shame that our great game could not keep their assets and personalities. What is it about hockey that causes us to lose some of our greatest practicioners? Are they seen to be too rebellious, or is it a fact that many of the National Associations have not been able to handle and accept these more professional members of the hockey family?

Wayne Diesel, Physiotherapist; From a Springbok to a Hotspur!

Clockwise from Top Left:
1 The Eye Doctor on the S.A. Training Field

2 Tony Blair welcomes the World Champions

3 Sherylle with England Coach, Sir Clive Woodward

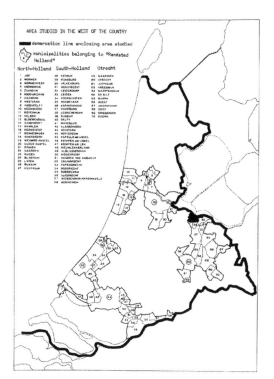

The Growth of "Hockey Municipalities" in Randstad Holland, 1960-1970

Population Densities; Note the expansion in the outer fringes of the 1960's Randstad.

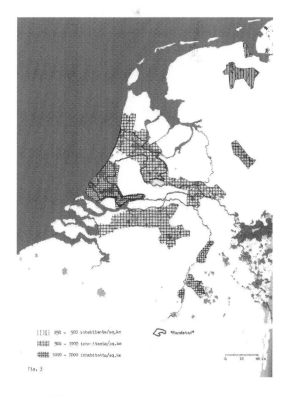

Fig. 3

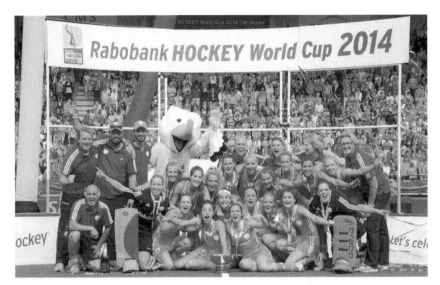

Another Gold for the Netherlands

Crowds and publicity - Hockey's Greatest Challenge

-Part K-
Hockey's New Shangri-La

After an earlier visit to Schevinengen as an English junior, the author here had become intrigued by its association with the concept and the region named Randstad Holland. This area bordered by Amsterdam and Utrecht in the north and Rotterdam and the Hague on its south-western margins left an open pastoral heartland, which in time an urban development would encircle as rapid economic growth took off to unprecedented heights.

It was an urban planner's dream. In post-war Netherlands, with much of the Rhine delta devastated by the effects of bombing, destruction and decay, the new professionals in the management of ports, transport and housing got to work to initiate some kind of a recovery. Rotterdam, in particular, was hardest hit as Holland's and Europe's outlet from the Meuse and Rhine's river systems. In short, if Europe was to recover, it all had to start and succeed in the Dutch ports of Amsterdam and Rotterdam.

The northern sector arc of Haarlem to Amsterdam to Utrecht not only had to rediscover its tourism, agricultural processing and educational functions, it also had to provide a new lease of life for the burgeoning light industrial growth that would accompany the huge American investment into the Marshall Plan's financing of Europe's recovery. The governmental city of The Hague would attract international organisations to function equally alongside the internal civic service base. The city began to flourish with increasing Dutch and foreign nationals requiring extra housing and related facilities at its edges, pushing urban sprawl into the previous hamlets of Wassenaar and Schevinengen.

Yet, the real push for growth was in the recovery of the giant, Rotterdam. New post war oil terminals with the emergent technological addition of containerisation shifted all trade activities from Dordrecht in the heart of the city downstream to the massive Europoort complex. Clearly an aptly named concentration of oil and petro- chemical industries sprouted up on a vast track of land to the West of the city, and it was here where the resurgence of the continent's economy gained ground as it gradually switched from coal to oil and gas for its industrial and domestic energy.

This emphasis on development was dynamic in the extreme as it demanded specific skills to handle the specialised industries and their derivatives around the rim of Randstad, which remember, was serving trade between the open sea and mainland Europe. There developed a highly skilled professional workforce to meet the demands of such rapid growth in the three decades that followed the Second World War. This period saw ports like Rotterdam, Amsterdam and Hamburg totally outstrip pre-war dominant rivals like Glasgow, Liverpool and London in their transition to modern technologies.

Rural depopulation from the outer fringes of the Netherlands flocked to Randstad Holland, and whilst the planners retained the agricultural heart of West Holland, there was a marked increase in the urban structure around its fringes. The oil-related activities, refining and processing, along with the derivative plastics sector were balanced by the more administrative and managerial employment bases in centres like The Hague and Utrecht. The Dutch economy boomed as it basically handled and processed Europe's and the world's natural resources.

So, what on earth had all this to do with hockey!? Simply put, it had always been the case in Europe that hockey had established its place amongst the confines of the educational middle classes of Germany, Britain, Spain, Belgium and the Netherlands. A typical hockey family had in the way of parents, lawyers, doctors, managers and consultants on all things commercial and financial. This sector thrived in the recovery of the 1950's and 1960's Randstad. It was solid and stable for the upbringing of children, and on the urban fringes of Haarlam, Amsterdam, Utrecht and Rotterdam, they were all connected in their joint aspirations in a rapidly expanding economy.

In summary, a huge middle class was growing more affluent by the decade and by the early 70's it was demanding more possibilities outside the workplace for their leisure time. There followed growth in family membership to sports clubs with fields and clubhouses that offered opportunities for all the family alike. Essentially, a new Hockey Shangri-La had emerged to dominate the core of the sport for some time to come in the Netherlands and North-West Europe as a whole. Why hockey? It was totally the suburban growth game whilst the less stable transient city centres were left to Ajax in Amsterdam and Feyenoord in Rotterdam, the football meccas of the nation.

By the 1970's it was no accident that the Dutch hockey club like their football counterparts was on the crest of a wave in European and world competition. Notable clubs like Klein Switzerland and HDM and HGC of the Hague, Amsterdam H.C. in Amstelveen and Kampong in Utrecht were flying high in the new Europa Cup events. This trend has continued down through the years as both Bloemendaal and Rotterdam took club hockey to a new dimension in Europe.

As expanding employment drifted upstream from Rotterdam into a hinterland that included Breda, S'Hertenbosch, Tilburg and Eindhoven, Randstad's 'body' had grown 'legs'. Indeed, the modern era of its contribution to hockey had been immense and has reflected the success that emanated from Randstad Holland and its effects were so widely felt that its tentacles even spread across nearby international borders onto Nord-Rhein Westfalia in Germany and into hockey resurgent Belgium via Brussels and Antwerp. (See map on page 171)

We must examine in detail to gain an understanding how this limited land area has bypassed and superseded the old British Empire's influences to completely dominate the game of hockey on the world stage by the year of 2015.

What a coup! How did they achieve all this in just two or three decades whilst the power blocks of Britain, Asia, Australia and the Latin world just stood idly by?

Both inside and beyond the Netherlands, there has always been a concentration of attention on the merits of the playing side of the sport of hockey. Understandably there is a wealth of evidence of the continuing medal haul at all levels that have coexisted with the aforementioned economic growth of a rich and influential middle-class. Not only was there expansion on the outer fringe of the Randstad in Western Holland, but soon after 1980, populations shifted along the Southern and Eastern zones of its border.

Light industries even pertinent to hockey were springing up like Desso, the synthetic turf leader with the accompanying yarn giant Ten Cate alongside hockey equipment groups like Brabo reflecting the rising employment of the province of Brabant.

Desso, in particular, based at the town of Oss, close to S'Hertonbosch, stepped into the light in the early 1980's as the nation's sand engineering expertise transferred into the realms of artificial hockey and football pitches. Consistent with the close co-operation of cross border business, the actual carpets were manufactured in Dendemonde in Belgium.

Yet, there was a real desire to set an overpowering dominance of the Dutch sporting market. The group was led by the enterprising Hans de Roij who shrewdly surrounded himself with a team of four excellent salesmen who had backgrounds in business and yes, in the playing of hockey at weekends. A staff with MBA qualifications and a knowledge of hockey clubs was quite clearly to have a huge advantage in approaching many of the comfortable, if not affluent local Councils during the formative years of the new fibre!

Herein was Holland's little secret. The Councils paid for the great majority of these pitches and insisted that the clubs could retain the revenues from the facilities. This effectively gave the ownership of the surfaces to the hockey clubs. When you own something yourself, you are more likely to look after it, a lesson that unfortunately was lost on the Councils' counterparts over in the United Kingdom where confusion reigned when Councils would allow the misuse of the surfaces and treat them as a cash cow for a variety of conflicting sports. The facilities over there were soon trashed, while the Dutch idea of cost to the Council, but ownership and maintenance to the club, really was an all-round winner for hockey in Randstad, Holland.

Desso did not stand idly by as they procured a lasting relationship with Heijmans, their partner construction company. They would be guided by the relevant Council to existing land that was available near to well established hockey clubs where there was no issue of changing the land use function as nearly all the turf fields were to be built over a lava base with the Sportilux carpet specified with appropriate sand infill on top of the original natural grass. Quality control was achieved and sanctioned by the Dutch Olympic group in testing the facility.

The yarn and overall carpet finish was to be of a high standard, even if many of these pitches only comprised of a one and a half metre run-off. The F.I.H. was not to sanction any international play on these surfaces therefore, which suited and reinforced the clubs ownership and control of their facilities. When these clubs required more synthetic pitches, they simply negotiated with the Councils for a share cost arrangement which again was a reminder of how Dutch hockey authorities worked together to meet the needs of a widely expanding sport. Well into the 1990's Desso's success story continued in pitch construction until that inevitable quest to service other countries and continents with their expertise meant that the earlier personal service from recognisable figures was spread too thin. Did they drop the ball? Maybe, but competition was fierce in the form of Lano and Tarket carpets, and emerging companies like Edelgrass, and much later, Greenfields, to share in the spoils. The overwhelming presence of Ten Cate which had all along produced yarn of a high quality and in abundance to order, was there waiting in the wings to dominate the industry.

Desso moved quickly to merge with another cross border co-operation with the Deutsche Linoleum Works (D.L.W.). The Germany giant based in Stuttgart already financed the building of tennis courts with an infrastructure and management group that dwarfed Desso. Yet the Dutch group still possessed multiple tufting machines, a recognised hockey carpet in Sportilux and of course the name of Desso.

On the merger, Desso insisted that three conditions had to be put in place. Firstly any compensation to be settled, secondly that Desso jobs had to be retained, but most importantly, the gift of a single bicycle from the Germans to the Dutch!! This was a lighthearted symbolic gesture as the Dutch had never known where all their bikes had disappeared to in the closing stages of World War II as the Germans retreated.

However Desso tried, as the new century dawned, Ten Cate was buying up or supporting the smaller turf companies and with the marketing and strategy of the world product of AstroTurf USA, DessoDLW slowly lost market share as the business fragmented losing the battle to the Dutch giants to competitors more sensitive and detailed in the modern marketing of a broad range of L.S.R., Polyethylene and Water turf products.

The situation started to mirror other developments in the devolution from Randstad in several areas of the nation's hockey. No longer the property of the west, gradually the National teams were drawing players from the expanding cities of Tilburg, Breda, Den Bosch and Eindhoven. The Dutch had evolved into a multicentric entity, rather like Germany, and hockey just grew and grew as there never was a barrier to players representing their county from outlying districts. The Netherlands was strong because its talent had become diversified. Easy, you might say, in a nation as small as Holland, but so many of the so called elite countries could learn this lesson from the Dutch.

One sector still remained constant in line with the success of the National teams and the commercial heads of Turf and sports equipment, and that was the supporting sponsors at all levels. Multi-nationals clearly with many hockey 'specialists' on their pay roll paved the way to provide a very solid platform for Dutch players and clubs to enter the professional playing era with no fears. Banks like Amro and Rabobank, oil and petrochemical giants like Royal Dutch Shell, and automobile conglomerates BMW and Volvo all played a major part in bringing top International hockey to full stadiums in Amstelveen and Rotterdam during the last two decades.

More significant was the care they have displayed for the sport at home, where they have put their muscle behind club hockey which still rules the roost in the priorities for the game in the Netherlands. The National Federation (The K.N.H.B.) has skilfully recognised the value of the Club, unfortunately forgotten today in several parts of the world. The K.N.H.B. has been a constant in the game advocating its commitment to the combined sport of men and women's hockey as it has staged the first dual World Cup in 1998. Not only that, but it also worked with Desso to hold Hockey's Premier event on water filled pitches built on top of a major football club's grass in just six weeks! Football stadiums for Hockey World Cups, only in Holland! They repeated the Utrecht experience in 1998 by hosting the successful World Cup in The Hague in 2014 along exactly the same lines.

The hockey dynamic here was and is an integrated one. Whereas in many of our previous chapters where individuals or individual circumstances led to localised hockey initiatives and development, here in the Netherlands it all expanded together from the Randstad. There has always been a concerted, combined effort to link human potential to technological innovation in environments that were rapidly extending themselves in and out of hockey and sport. The Dutch have allowed the early assets of the Randstad to spread its influence even beyond the national borders. If ever there was proof of a total team effort, just look no further than the communities here that have made hockey a lifestyle.

Whilst the Netherlands prospered in the sport's broadening appeal and commercial outlets, it did by no means dominate all sectors of hockey. Its tentacles had pushed south and east, influencing the direction that Belgium would take in the recent decade for sure, but eastwards into Germany it was slightly a different story. The great rivalry between the two hockey super powers would continue to this day as both parties literally sparred with each other in some areas whilst, as we have seen, sharing their expertise to great effect in other parts of the sport.

The Germans are misunderstood! That line has been often quoted as sports critics have widely labelled the nation that has won so consistently at world level as predictable, spectator unfriendly, and methodical at best.

Really? The same nation that produced the Zellers, Blocher, Michael Green and Natasha Keller have been the very country that have won more Junior and Senior World Cup gold medals than any other. It was Germany that also built a production line of visionary world coaches that included Horst Wein, Paul Lissek, and Bernard Peters.

Inevitably the Germans would be rather nonplussed by the assertion that it was only Randstad Holland's extension that spurred the growth of the game in Germany. There is ample evidence to show that the adjacent Nord-Rhein Westphalia and the Rhein cities of Dusseldorf and Cologne have been key focal points to hockey's success in Germany just across the border from the Netherlands. Even the National stadium has been located in a town the closest to the Dutch border in Monchengladbach. The German motivation revolved around the confidence that any international tournament would attract a double audience with huge numbers pouring in from Holland.

The current German Director of Performance, Heino Knuf, reflects this concentration of activity in his own personal hockey history. He was a solid central defender back in the 70's and early 80's at Swartz-Weiss Koln where he laid the foundations for a future career in coaching as he rose through the ranks to guide Junior World Cup teams to National success. Surprisingly, Heino outlines what is important to the average hockey enthusiast,

"Firstly, we do not here in Deutschland want to see the game go professional. We value the family of hockey too much. As soon as money, agents and contracts start to dominate, we will lose the social dimension in the game with its unique set of networking which we all currently enjoy. Our federation thrives upon these relationships between players, our administration and the commercial ties that allow our top players to perform at International level for near on a decade. We have bankers, doctors, teachers and lawyers, and we are proud of the fact that they can play in our National teams.

It is our duty to encourage and maintain these links in hockey that go far beyond the competitive stage. They also bind all the layers of hockey together from the lower club player to the double Olympian. Our clubs reflect this interconnection which by its very nature creates role models for our young players. This continual awareness of the next generation is central to our philosophy as we have, don't forget, 46,000 players registered of which 28,000 are boys and girls. There is next to no hockey in schools, and it falls upon us to introduce the sport as early as five years old into our club structure!!

You English have got it so wrong, you have always started, eh, at ten or eleven, far too late. Gavin for instance, when did you start playing football?"

"I was playing like Beckenbauer when I was five!!", I said.

"I told you, you were always better at football!! So now you know why."

Heino had a point in his enthusiasm for the kindergarten. The German experience started young by encouraging the hand and foot movements alone associated with hockey, and perhaps most of all, by stressing the hockey balance the young players would need as they took to the introduction of small team games later. Suffice to say, basic skills had to be specifically taught to the age and stage of the child,

"We learn the game, like we learn life, in stages. At our clubs each new skills set follows the previous lessons like chapters in a book. It sounds obvious, but we do not look at the overhead pass till later in their development. The skills to be learned reflect the stage of the young player's physical and emotional development."

The reader may not be surprised by the organised approach of how young Germans acquire a range of skills at a higher level of consistent execution, say, than their British counter parts. So often I have observed, as a coach, school or junior club games at youth level in England where I was very impressed by the levels of technical skill of a particular individual, only to be later told that the sixteen year old was a German import.

In fact, many German imports have parents who have sent their sons and daughters across the water to learn how to speak the English language, but end up mainly acquiring the fighting sports spirit of the Brits!

"We love it, it makes us scream and shout, and it is the focal point that all German Hockey is based on!"

What was Heino talking about? Germans, emotional, loving every minute of it? It was, in effect, one aspect of hockey that had even passed over the 'Randstad neighbours'. It was, Indoor Hockey!

The German experience with the indoor version of the sport had been unique. Its climate of harsh winters allied to the prevalence of indoor sports arenas and schools which have been purpose built to accommodate the needs of a host of indoor activities, have made its sportsmen and women very attached to the Indoor game. Note that German winters are by nature nearly six months long, and the decision to play indoors with the rules constructed in Germany, have been in evidence for over six decades. Indeed, the expression of the game internationally had been much slower as the Germans hardly lost a game during this period. Only in German-speaking nations was there any competition.

It is true to recognise that this element of the sport was the missing link from our extended Randstad core. Whilst the Dutch looked to the open spaces associated with synthetic pitch development and its ensuing commercial sponsorships which had allowed national team players in winter to travel to warm weather training sites in the sun, the Germans always counter-claimed the advantages of the technical and competitive values associated with indoor hockey.

Any study of a German hockey player would reveal the theme of definition in the precision of their basic skills. In Indoor hockey there is little room for errors in a restricted area of play, and rules which deny the third dimension, the lifting of the ball outside the shooting circles. Angles and speed of pass are all important factors in this game and possession is nine tenths of the law. Personal qualities of patience and restraint are the equal here to individual flair and dynamism. Some cynics would say that is why the Germans reign supreme, whilst the Dutch remain excellent but relatively apathetic toward the game.

This open air argument is worth stressing in contrast between the two nations. Within the outdoor game, the Dutch still place due emphasis on fluidity and risk with open wide build up zones to launch their attacks with only a passing tolerance to defensive details and principles. It is the opposite with their German neighbours who thrive on security and stability of the ball when under their control. In short, they are tighter in or out of possession. Heino certainly espoused these beliefs in the way he emphasised the importance of a defensive marking platform when his teams had conceded possession and required a safe midfield built around secure passing and receiving options to gain optimum field positions.

With the noted excitement of Bundesliga Indoor matches and playoffs between November and April where big games can attract thousands of spectators and television coverage, it is here where the German hockey framework has been carefully constructed over the years. The overlap between youth and indoor hockey has been inseparable with a groundswell of continuity and popularity between the two parties. Young

Germans play inside, just look at the other popular sports of volleyball, basketball, and handball, all often played at the same facilities as indoor hockey.

Heino moved the conversation around to an area of great concern to him and it did involve how the indoor game would fit into the demands of an ever-increasing hockey calendar. Indeed, and with no excuses, he attributed Germany's relatively poor showing in the 2014 World Cup to the over cluttered F.I.H. tournament agendas thrown at the national associations in modern hockey,

"It is something that we must address rapidly. The F.I.H. now is asking national teams within eight months to perform at World Cups, Champions Trophies, and Indoor World Cups. Remember that is going alongside Bundesliga Club hockey, the E.H.L. and the newly founded Indian Hockey League Franchise. Something has to give in terms of quality of play displayed at this level. Most of our top players are still not full-time athletes today, so we have to contend with non-availabilities as a result of examinations and work schedules. We try to manage this overload, but it is the players that are suffering the most. Can we sustain a world position in the top four for the foreseeable future? This could be in doubt as we are under considerable pressure from the recovering Asian nations, a new quality of play in the Southern hemisphere from Argentina and New Zealand, and here in Europe by huge Government investment programmes in Great Britain and Belgium."

Belgium? Even the Germans have been wary of the strides this small country has made over the last decade. The national team has emerged as a top four country in Europe and a top six nation worldwide in just under a decade, and that is just part of the story.

The Dynamic of the influence of Randstad Holland pushing south through Breda and Brabant province down into the sleepy hockey enclaves of Antwerp and Brussels took time, as Belgium once a top nation with a powerful F.I.H. president Rene Frank, lost its grip after 1980 for literally two decades. The country just went missing at World Cups and Olympics with plummeting numbers playing the game as standards slipped. However, after the 2000 Olympics in Sydney, there was literally a growing scale of movement in terms of hockey players and coaches taking advantage of the free labour laws within the European Community.

By 2004, Irish, Spanish, and French players were spotted in Belgian club line- ups beside a constant flow of players from the Southern Hemisphere seeking overseas experiences away from the institutes and academies down under. Aussie coaches like Colin Batch and Adam Commins were spreading their wings to absorb European conditions but equally to influence the playing culture of Europe's sleeping giants. Whilst Belgium was sleeping, the Netherlands and Germany had moved onto another plane through this period in whatever area of the game one chose to look.

Despite these developments in cross continental playing and coaching, there was an awakening within Belgium that something had to be done to rescue the game there, as even the F.I.H. Headquarters in 2006, always in Brussels, was removed from its Belgium base to Switzerland. Was this the last straw for the Belgians?

Hockey was to respond very positively after the nation's Olympic committee concluded that it could, in that group of sports, head towards a medal potential in the world's major events, if only the Government agencies could release funding to grant aid to the athletes and the clubs. Increased funding would normally be directed at active youth programmes at the one end of development, whilst promoting higher performance levels at the other end in international contests.

The hiring of experienced coaches and specialists at club level has been prevalent since 2006, and since then a major coup was achieved in attracting the services of Dutch master coach Marc Lammers. In effect, that one appointment reflected the drive and new ambition that the Belgium Federation had at this stage as they recognised that young players at last had role models that they could look up to and respect.

The role that the clubs took up was also pivotal. Clubs and the National Governing body had for sometime been consulting with the likes of Heino Knuf just across the border in how the Germans had placed their priorities on the development of young players in clubs and with a well structured coaching system which enhanced their emergence into junior National team players. Equally, they had taken note of the relationships that Dutch clubs had formed with their commercial sponsors and media expertise.

These two vital elements were absorbed by Belgian clubs with their federations backing at the very time when the European Hockey League (E.H.L.) was formed in 2006. So there appeared a timely sweetener, and the theatre for the improving clubs such as Royal Leopold, Dragons and Waterloo Ducks to continue their progress in the higher levels of competition. At last, Belgium clubs had the stimulus of potential titles in mind and their response was to mount a serious search for young stars across Europe.

Did they come from Germany and Holland? No, the cream of the hockey neighbouring elite remained at home before the eyes of national coaches and their requirements for squad training. However, Belgium was viewed differently by nations who were not providing the necessary internal competition in their own countries, differently that is, by their ambitious players.

Two such players, since 2012, have tested the Belgian waters, one a Spanish Indoor international goal keeper, the other a young England striker already established in the English team. Cristian Penalba had met his intended club hierarchy at Eindhoven airport to discuss the possibility of playing at the Royal Antwerp club. In Terrassa he had been a stable player for five years, and was recommended by friends to break away from a limited and predictable Spanish League in terms of its hockey depth.

"I wanted the competition. In Spain I was active for Atletico Terrassa for just one game in four. The sponsorships were drying up and here was a chance to conduct junior coaching at Antwerp along with a paid position in a league which was gaining respect for its quality and competitiveness. Of the twelve teams, in the Premier Division, seven or eight of the games were very tight in encounters for me as the Antwerp goalkeeper. Unbelievably, such was my form that I have been, at thirty-two years old, been called up for Outdoor National team training with Spain. Our club squad, of eighteen, included four Spaniards, two Australians, and one Canadian, and with sponsors like Deutsche Bank, and crowds of such rare enthusiasm, all the weekend games are festive occasions."

A similar story greeted the England striker Alistair Brogdon when he was attracted to play a season in 2013 at Waterloo Ducks. The same theme of an attachment to taking junior team training alongside his own training base of three evenings a week pushed him to the limit. His motivation for the Brussels hockey life revealed the desire to play under new methods of coaching and a varied training emphasis. He was not disappointed when this was reinforced by Belgian Pascal Kira and New Zealander Shane McCleod,

"There was a different emphasis at Ducks, more ball work and an encouraging coaching ideology to use these skills all over the field. Our players were comfortable on the ball in most tight situations, and if Pascal epitomised that style, then Shane kept the balance with more concerted defensive disciplines. Yet I was left with an impression of wide ranging sponsorship support, large vociferous crowds and a coaching system that

184

viewed individualism as a strength. The Premier League with its top four play- off games at the end of each season held both intensity, local pride and enjoyment. I left Brussels a better player."

Belgium has often been regarded as a crossroads of Western Europe and in hockey terms, lying between Holland and Germany, it has at last deliberately taken advantage of the close ties and benefited from the development and cohesion of the three countries. Today with open borders, the differences must be examined more closely as they have merged ever tighter. It was not only in ideas, transport, and commercial links that have bound this overgrown Randstad. At the 2012 Olympics, it was first place for Germany, Bronze for the Netherlands and 5th for Belgium in the men's event, a 1, 3, and 5 for an area of land (including just the German margins) of only 150 square miles!

Arguably, Belgium had benefited most from this mecca of hockey involvement and exchange. My contention that these three nations cannot really be considered separately anymore. Their integration covers former top F.I.H. Dutch umpire Pete Von Reth assuming the title of Umpire coordinator for Germany, as well as the transfers of talented Belgium players like ace striker Tom Boon playing at Bloemendaal in Holland. Meanwhile, both Dutch and Belgium clubs have shown mounting interest in Germany's Indoor programme as the F.I.H. inaugurates the Indoor World Cup as a permanent event.

It started as a planning idea, Randstad Holland, as early as half a century ago, and it has grown almost like a human life. In hockey terms, it initiated hockey stadiums and the dynamic new surfaces which have attracted world events and tournaments. As it expanded, it staged magnificent sporting exhibitions at the Koln Messe and major world Indoor events for hockey. All these infrastructural assets attracted the real human interest in the form of coaching ideas, commercial support systems and organisational control from international bodies like the F.I.H. and the E.H.F. Their quest for publicity and media exposure has been ongoing with increasing stress on the marketing process to launch and protect our sport well into the 21st century.

Still, more than all of this, the small sector of North- West Europe has brought achievement and success for one of the world's most inclusive sports, for young and old, for men and women, and for spectator alike. Hockey grew out of this region replacing older, more tired parts of the world. As intimated, Randstad's child came screaming into the early 1970's to blossom into adulthood in the three succeeding decades.

Now its connective web sits comfortably on the mature side of middle age, still guiding hockey through the challenges of an ever decreasing world size where loyalty to sporting traditions is often contested. Throughout this life, hockey has responded so positively to the changing world. Its journey across the continents required a true affinity to dynamism. As a young entity hockey passed all the tests. Now, will it show equally the wisdom of longevity?

Index

A

Aggiss, Richard 54, 105, 141, 142
AHA 104, 105, 106
Ahmad, Shabaz 91, 125
Annan, Alison 112
Applebee, Constance 24, 93
AstroTurf iii, 12, 28, 33, 34, 35, 36, 38, 39, 40, 41, 42, 43, 44, 48, 61, 111, 177
AWHA 104, 105, 106

B

Barnett, Simon 128, 130
Barber, Paul 54, 119
Barton, Nick 122, 123, 124, 125
Bell, David 107
Bloemendaal vii, 88, 89, 90, 91, 92, 93, 94, 175, 185
Bloomfield, John 106
Boddington, Bill 2
Boon, Tom 91, 185
Bovelander, Floris Jan 91
Brinkman, Jacques 92
Brogdon, Alistair 184

C

Cadman, John 69, 70, 71, 72, 73, 74, 75, 81
Calder, Sherylle 151, 160, 163, 166
Calzado, Juan 86
Cambridge 21, 22, 23, 24, 27, 30, 69, 70, 74
Chand, Dhyan 1, 2, 3, 4, 8, 19
Charlesworth, Ric 19, 54, 107, 112, 117, 121, 125, 165
Clarke, Trevor 73
Cockett, John 22
Coles, Allan 106
Cooke, Sean 20
Cooper, Denys 36
Cullis, Bill 123, 124

D

Davidson, Bob 141
Davies, Craig 107, 121
De Roij, Hans 176
Deans, Brent 107, 113, 115
Deo, Santiago 86, 87

Desso 39, 42, 43, 175, 176, 177, 178
Diesel, Wayne 151, 154, 156, 157, 166
Dodds, Richard 19, 22
Dwyer, Jamie 25, 91, 96

E

Europa Cup 142, 175

F

Faaronheigt, Steven 49, 52, 53, 60, 61
Featherstone, Gavin i, 51, 52, 53, 54, 55, 56, 59, 60, 96, 143, 144, 151, 153, 166
FIH 1, 9, 11, 12, 25, 27, 28, 34, 36, 38, 39, 43, 44, 48, 59, 64, 71, 89, 95, 103, 124, 125, 167
Fletcher, Robin 71
Frank, Renee 1, 36, 182

H

Haslehurst, Peter 107
Hawkes, Rochelle 112
Hendricks, Mauritz 145
Hensel, Jos 145
Hobkirk, Alan 34, 35
Hudson, Nicky 112
Hurst, John 124

I

IFWHA 27
Irvine, Jim 54

J

Jackson, Craig 20
James, Jimmy 7
Jaspan, Steve 151
Junior World Cup 9, 12, 97, 109, 179

K

Kentwell, Jun 95, 101
Kentwell, Richard 95, 141
Kerly, Sean 19, 54
Khehar, Sutinder 7
Kira, Pascal 184
Knowles, Mark 96
Knuf, Heino 179, 183
Kruize, Ties 89, 121

L

Lammers, Marc 183
Lejeune, Lisanne 89
Livingstone, Craig 151, 166, 169
Lombi, Jorge 96
Loughborough Colleges 69, 70, 71

M

McCloed, Shane 184
McMurray, Clive 144
Menzies, Graeme 22, 24
Michalaro, Brad 20
Milner, Ed 34, 35, 36, 38, 40, 42, 43, 44, 61
Monsanto 33, 35, 38, 41
Murray, Frank 105, 112

N

Nash, Graham 139, 141, 143, 144
Nehru Tournament 8
Neuber, Joe 97, 99, 100
Nogareda, Manuel 84

O

OBO 128, 129, 130, 132
O'Connor, Ray 139, 141, 144, 149
O'Haire, Jon 129
Olympics v, vii, 1, 2, 5, 6, 7, 8, 11, 17, 19, 22, 28, 34, 35, 49, 50, 51, 52, 53, 54, 55, 70, 75, 85, 86, 87, 92, 95, 103, 106, 110, 111, 112, 115, 116, 120, 121, 124, 125, 127, 129, 140, 141, 148, 151, 152, 153, 158, 160, 165, 167, 169, 176, 183

P

Pappin, Veryan 124
Penalba, Cristian 184
Pereira, Charles 20
Peters, Bernard 179
Pleshakov, Vladimir 119
Polo Club 76, 83, 84, 85, 86, 87, 100
Prior, Don 139, 140, 141, 143, 144
Pullen, Robbie 20

R

Randstad 171, 173, 174, 175, 176, 177, 178, 179, 180, 181, 182, 185
Rundle, Percy 22
Rylett, Kevin 54

S

Self, Roger 105, 121, 141
Shaw, John 96, 122, 123
Simpson, Sharyn 112
Singh Bhogal, Kuldip 6, 7
Singh Saini, Balwant 6
Singh Sandhu, Rajinder 5, 6, 7
Spice, Chris 113, 116
Stacey, Jay 91
Stiles, Bob 120, 121, 129
Stott, Pauline 115
Swann, Mathew 91

T

Tattershall, Roger 71
Taylor, Ian 54, 119, 120, 121, 122, 124, 125, 126, 131

V

Vans Agnew, Bill 70
Van T'Hek, Tommy 89, 93
Van Wyck, Remco 91
Vinson, David 122, 127
Von Heumann, Wim 105
Von Reth, Peter 142, 144

W

Walsh, Terry 54, 107, 121
Walter, Cyril 4, 68
WC Eagles 95, 96, 97, 98, 101
Wein, Horst 74, 75, 76, 77, 78, 79, 80, 81, 105, 179
Whitaker, David 54, 60, 61
Wigmore, Stan 71
Woodward, Clive 163, 164

Bibliography

Wein, Horst. The Science of Hockey, 1975. Print.

Walter, Cyril. Hockey, The Gold Medal Way, 1989. Print.

Olympic Athlete Program - Making Great Australians. Australian Government Sports Policy, Australian Sports Commission 1994. Print.

Taylor, Ian. Behind the Mask, 1989. Print.

The Randstad; The Urbanised Zone of the Netherlands. Ministry of Housing and Physical Planning, 1970. Print.

Lawrence, G.R.P. Randstad Holland,1973. Print.

Kuper, Simon and Szymanski, Stefan. Soccernomics, 2012. Print.

Hopcroft, Arthur. The Football Man, 1969. Print.

Whitaker, David. The Hockey Workshop, 1992. Print.

Astroturf and How it Grew; Invention and Technology Magazine, Issue 4, 2005.

VIDEO LIBRARY

Hockey for Goalkeepers 1986
Hockey, The Modern Game 1987
Hockey for Umpires 1989
Hockey for Coaches 1990
Hockey ; The Tactical Game 1992
Hooked on Hockey ; 1995
Keeper 2000 ; 1996
Hockey Down Under,2002
Hockey Goes Dutch, 2004
Hockey Zindabad 2005

All Titles directed by Gavin Featherstone.

About the Author

A coach with a wide-range of experiences, Featherstone has 324 international matches to his credit as a former Olympic coach for both the United States (1984) and South Africa (1996). At the 1984 games, he was the youngest coach to ever take a field hockey team to the Olympics. He also led the USA in the Pan-American games, while heading up South Africa in the World Cup and All-African games. Featherstone has also served as the head coach for England's men's and women's U21 World Cup teams.

An outstanding tactician, Featherstone has produced 20 DVDs endorsed by the International Hockey Federation (FIH), which have been distributed worldwide to more than 25 countries to teach strategies and principles of field hockey. He has also been selected in the past to lead several world seminars by the FIH in the use of video breakdown and film study by athletes to improve performance on the pitch.

As a player, Featherstone competed for Durham University, where he captained the first field hockey club in school history, eventually becoming President of the Durham University Athletic Union, and played hockey for the British Universities Team. Featherstone then went on to play in England's national program, where he was team captain at all levels and played in both the World and European Cups.

He received a Bachelors of Arts degree from Durham in 1975 before earning a Postgraduate Certificate of Education from Oxford University in 1976.

Look for this upcoming book, also by Gavin Featherstone:

That Ain't Hockey

Goodbye Chelsea to a life in hockey

Coming November 2015